VANISHED DENVER LANDMARKS

VANISHED DENVER LANDMARKS

MARK A. BARNHOUSE

Published by The History Press
Charleston, SC
www.historypress.com

First published 2021

Manufactured in the United States

ISBN 9781467148405

Library of Congress Control Number: 2021943425

CONTENTS

PREFACE

Buildings break your heart, especially when you invest them with your ideas and your identity—especially when you make them symbols not just of who you are but of who you are supposed to be.
—*Tom Junod*[1]

Those words are about a particular building after a particular event, but they are just as applicable to Denver's vanished landmarks. The buildings in this book—hotels, houses, office buildings, even sanitaria—were each invested with meaning by their builders and inhabitants, not to mention the many Denverites who encountered them every day until suddenly they were gone. Some buildings everyone knew, probably entering them many times over their lives, while others were private, even obscure.

My interest in an older Denver started at an early age. My mother loved the vast mansions built by nineteenth- and early twentieth-century magnates that once ran uninterruptedly down Sherman, Grant and Logan Streets. She remembered how, when she first arrived as a teenager in 1938, she could walk under a shade canopy from her house in Congress Park all the way downtown where she had a job making candy. She moved from one house to another, her builder father converting old Denver Squares into apartments or rooming houses. She inherited her love of old buildings from him, Lester Frederick Smith, whose name comes up later in this book. Growing up in the 1970s, I heard her frequent plaint, "They might just as well tear down everything, they've destroyed so much already." Christmas gifts of

Signage announcing the property owner's request to have The Hut at 1980 Albion Street declared "Non-Historic," a precursor to demolition. *Courtesy Angel Johnson and Erik Stark.*

photograph-filled books further stimulated my interest: Sandra Dallas's *Yesterday's Denver*, and *Denver: A Pictorial History* by William C. Jones and Kenton Forrest. The garage sale discovery of a 1959 *Denver Post* rotogravure supplement, *This Is Colorado*, published to commemorate "Rush to the Rockies," the Pikes Peak Gold Rush's centennial, continued my fascination with a Denver I never knew. The results of these sojourns are the several books I have published with Arcadia Publishing and The History Press.

Choosing landmarks for this book was not easy. I had previously published *Lost Denver*, covering over one hundred old buildings. Others have also published books on the theme. I decided that rather than try to rehash what historians have done before, I would seek out some less well-known ones—which is not to say that this book lacks all of the old warhorses. The selection is eclectic rather than comprehensive, and during the research and writing, I became fascinated with each one as I discovered things about them I had not known before.

Just prior to this book's completion, History Colorado announced it had digitized the two volumes of its 1920s Denver Ku Klux Klan ledgers, making them available on its website (historycolorado.org/kkkledgers). A Denver newspaperman had donated them in 1946, and due to their explosive nature, the historical society had kept fairly quiet about their existence until the 1970s. Historians have been able to study them in person, but the convenience of online access should compel everyone to consult them whenever they research Denverites alive during that period. Searching for names discussed in this book, I found four (five, if you count Mayor Benjamin Stapleton, now the best-known Denver Klan member of all). These are Roy J. Dutton, the Republic Building's builder; Teller Ammons, son-in-law of Fred Davis and one-term Colorado governor; Clarence George Campbell of Knight-Campbell Music Company; and William D. Reynolds, founder of KLZ Radio. With some exceptions such as those just mentioned, Denver's upper crust did not join the Klan; it was largely a middle-class movement, as the ledgers' addresses reveal. Rather than rewrite the text, I include the names here. Think about them, and the pervasiveness of the Klan in Denver during the 1920s, as you read. Even better: look at the ledgers.[2]

Many people have helped me write this book. First, Amy Zimmer: I asked her if there were buildings she was unable to cover in her *Lost Denver* due to space constraints, and she sent me a long list. As a former member of the Denver Landmarks Preservation Commission, she also suggested highlighting more recent losses demolished by uncaring developers during Denver's twenty-first-century boom. Researching a book during a pandemic when libraries were closed proved no easy matter; Judy Stalnaker's recommendation of GenealogyBank.com's newspaper archives proved invaluable. Also deserving of many thanks for their help, advice and inspiration are Shaun Boyd, Katie Bush, Artie Crisp, Kellen Cutsforth, Ray Defa, Bob DeWitt, Roger Dudley, Debra Faulkner, Angel Johnson, Jori Johnson, Susan Keats, Leslie Mohr Krupa, Shari Myers, Dr. Thomas J. Noel, Mary O'Neil, Heather Ormsby, Hilary Parrish, the late Carl Sandberg, Laurie Simmons, Tom Simmons, Erik Stark and, as always, Matt Wallington.

INTRODUCTION

Historic preservation in Denver took off later than elsewhere. The concept dates to the 1850s—the decade of Denver's founding—when Virginian women worked to protect George Washington's Mount Vernon. Recognizing the importance of their city to the American story, in 1931, Charleston, South Carolina residents established America's first designated historic district. In 1935, President Franklin Roosevelt signed the Historic Sites Act, which led to the Historic American Buildings Survey, originally providing work to unemployed architects and other professionals during the Great Depression; it continues today under the National Park Service. In 1949, President Harry Truman signed legislation creating the National Trust for Historic Preservation, and in 1966, President Lyndon Johnson approved the National Historic Preservation Act, which created the National Register of Historic Places.

What was Denver doing during that time, when most white Americans believed in an unlimited future defined by material prosperity? While some appreciated historic buildings and neighborhoods and bemoaned the loss of every landmark that came down, they were in the minority. After World War II, following two decades when very little changed, Denver's business and political leaders, following the lead of out-of-town developers like New York's William Zeckendorf and Dallas's Murchison brothers, came to view their city as frumpy and old-fashioned, inhibiting Denver from competing with other cities to attract new business and residents. They decided to remake downtown, the main workplace for white suburbanites, who would arrive by automobile via wide new freeways. Old Capitol Hill mansions, built to lavish standards for an elite class that had moved on, had been converted to apartments, offices and even music schools—these, leaders hoped, would give way to luxury apartment towers. Most new structures that replaced them were mediocre (true now as well), and many treasures came down just for parking. Beautiful nineteenth-century schools, churches and houses were antithetical to this postwar vision. Advocates of "progress" lacked the imagination to understand that the precious old could peacefully coexist alongside the gleaming new, and even enhance it.

In 1958, the city established DURA, the Denver Urban Renewal Authority, initially focused on residential areas. "Slum" clearance was widespread nationally, the idea that decaying cities could be "healed" through wholesale demolition of "blight." The three quotation-marked words in the previous sentence were based on false ideas of what ailed cities. Residents, usually people of color, did not consider their neighborhoods, long red-lined by banks, blighted slums, and if any healing was to be done, it would have been better accomplished through community building than with bulldozers. Planners exacerbated, rather than healed, Denver's economic and racial divides. In the 1960s and 1970s, DURA turned its attention to downtown and the downtown-adjacent Auraria neighborhood, the city's oldest. Its Skyline Urban Renewal Project demolished all or part of a seventeen-block area of what was then called "lower downtown," roughly Speer Boulevard to 20th Street, Curtis Street to the alley between Larimer and Market Streets. Across Cherry Creek, DURA razed nearly everything between Speer Boulevard, Colfax Avenue and Wazee Street (now Auraria Parkway) for a three-institution campus; displaced residents were promised free college educations. DURA has since embraced historic preservation as a tool and has become better at respecting Denver's non-Anglo communities, but in its early decades, DURA served as an apparatus for Denver's moneyed interests to remake the city using since-disproven "clean slate" theories.

DURA was just part of Denver's self-destruction; private enterprise played a larger role. In his autobiography, Zeckendorf mocked Denver as a "sleepy, self-satisfied town," controlled by a coterie of twenty conservative, intermarried families that held it back.[3] But slowly at first, then accelerating in the 1960s and later, Denver's old guard either died off or avidly embraced the new ethos. Two financial institutions, Central Bank and the quintessentially old guard Colorado National Bank, bought nearby properties and demolished them, cleaning up their immediate environs in private urban renewal schemes. Developers, only rarely Denver-based,

A man signs the petition to save the Republic Building, 1981. *Thomas J. Noel collection; photograph by Roger Whitacre.*

flattened old properties one by one, a process that has continued unimpeded into the twenty-first century. Through it all, citizens wondered, if Europeans kept their old buildings for centuries, why were Americans so eager to demolish theirs?

One of DURA's main arguments for Skyline was economic: city services for old buildings cost more than they generated in tax receipts. While the projects that replaced the historic fabric produce more revenue, one wonders what would have happened had DURA's board listened to Helen Millet Arndt. In 1967, Denver chartered the Denver Landmarks Preservation Commission (DLPC), a nine-member volunteer body that recommends landmark designations. Arndt was its first chairperson, and she immediately created a list of buildings within Skyline that should be preserved for historical reasons. DURA ignored Arndt, its chair, attorney Alex Holland, claiming (incorrectly) that they were not historic, that developers preferred to work with clean slates and therefore 100 percent of Skyline's blocks must be razed. Yet had Arndt's listed buildings remained, they would have provided historic texture to a section of downtown that now sorely lacks it and would have forced architects to work around them, producing better, more humane designs than what ultimately resulted: a dead zone of dull skyscrapers and blank walls. Moreover, the historic buildings, surrounded by new ones, would likely have been renovated and repurposed, generating jobs and tax revenue, just as nearby Larimer Square and LoDo have done. The latter area, which began interesting preservationists in the 1970s, is a national model for adaptive reuse of old warehouse districts, its property values constantly rising.

We know historic preservation as an economic good, but some of its strongest advocates are aging and dying off. Some young people pursue degrees in preservation, but they, like preservationists before them, are a minority among their peers. As Denver's population has mushroomed in recent years, its median age has declined—Denver is now more of a young person's city than at any time since the 1860s. Few now recall preservation battles of the 1960s, 1970s and 1980s, when many fine buildings disappeared forever. The economic pressures are more intense in the twenty-first century as city living has become chic again—all those new arrivals need places to live. The purpose of this book is, therefore, to remind readers of Denver's vanished landmarks so that those that remain will still be around when Denver celebrates its 200th birthday in 2058.

Chapter 1
RESIDENTIAL LANDMARKS

Anderson House

The name "Anderson House" was in general use only during this dwelling's final years; for most of its history, it was simply 2329 Eliot Street. The fight to save it symbolized the losses of many similar houses—built for the middle and upper middle classes when Denver was young—demolished by developers, but this particular house had a great backstory. Attorney William W. Anderson did not build the two-story Queen Anne home but rented it between 1897 and 1904. In 1915, he bought it, living here until his 1930 death. In *Rediscovering Northwest Denver* (1976), Ruth Eloise Wiberg referred to it as "a tall house on a tall hill," a neighborhood landmark.

Anderson's claim to fame was brief, but it involved some of the best-known Denverites of his day: *Denver Post* publishers Frederick Gilmer Bonfils and Harry Heye Tammen, their star "sob sister" reporter "Polly Pry" (Leonel Ross O'Bryan) and a famous Cañon City penitentiary inmate, Alfred Packer, the "Colorado Cannibal." Bonfils and Tammen had made the *Post* into Denver's leading daily by emphasizing emotional, sometimes lurid stories, often using red ink on front-page headlines to add shock value. Their shared office, painted crimson, was called the "Red Room" officially and the "Bucket of Blood" by their enemies.

In 1900, Pry wrote a series of articles about Packer, who in 1874 had guided a hunting party in isolated Lake County. After several months, Packer emerged alone, and a rescue party found unmistakable signs that some of his companions had been eaten. Packer admitted consuming

The Anderson House, 2015. *Tom Simmons collection; photograph by Tom Simmons.*

their flesh after their deaths from starvation but denied killing them. Nevertheless, he was given a long sentence. Pry focused on injustice done to Packer, and her employers made freeing him a *cause celèbre*. Anderson, sensing potential glory and profit, announced he would meet with Packer. Traveling to Cañon City, he told Packer he was acting as Bonfils's and Tammen's personal representative (he was not) and persuaded him to pay twenty-five dollars as a "docket fee." The publishers were incensed by Anderson's unauthorized initiative and summoned him to their office. There, with Pry present, the men argued, with Pry attempting to mediate. Anderson reached inside his coat, pulled a gun and shot Bonfils several times. He left the room, returned, cornered Tammen and shot him several times. The blood was real now; while both men survived, Bonfils's wounds were nearly fatal. Not everyone thought of Anderson as the villain—Bonfils and Tammen had alienated many in their crusades—and after two mistrials, he was acquitted in a third trial.

In 2015, the house's owner accepted an offer from a developer who planned to replace it with eighteen townhomes. Aware of the history, neighborhood activist Rafael Espinoza, then running for city council, filed with the DLPC to preserve it, joined by neighbor Jerry Olson and others.

One DLPC commissioner, architectural historian Kathy Corbett, favored preservation: "If history isn't stories, what else do we have? The history of Denver, this kind of rough-and-tumble Western mythos, is a lot of what makes Denver what it is." City council disagreed, judging Anderson's connections to Bonfils, Tammen, Pry and Packer unimportant. The house came down.[4]

Belmar

Depression-era Denver saw two superlative, similarly named mansions erected, providing jobs to unemployed artisans. In 1932, Senator Lawrence Cowle Phipps built Belcaro, Italian for "beautiful, dear one," in southeast Denver, centerpiece of its eponymous neighborhood. In 1936–37, May Bonfils built Belmar in then-unincorporated Lakewood, near South Wadsworth Boulevard and West Alameda Avenue, but its name was not Italian. She was the daughter of *Denver Post* publisher Frederick Bonfils and his wife, Belle, and when May built her country palace, she named it for her mother, combining "Bel" with "Mar," a shortened form of Mary. Devoutly Catholic, she may have been honoring the Virgin Mother, but more likely, it was for herself, May being a form of Mary. Today, Belcaro remains Denver's finest mansion, while Belmar is lost, thanks to one unfortunate decision.

May suffered from extreme sibling rivalry with her six-years-younger sister, Helen. Perhaps that competitiveness led May to commission Denver's premier domestic architect, the École des Beaux-Arts–trained Jules Jacques Benoit Benedict, for her twenty-room manse while her sister remained in their parents' Humboldt Street home. May had enraged her father in 1904 when she married, at the age of twenty-one, Knight-Campbell piano salesman Clyde Berryman. He was not of their social class—but far worse, he was Protestant. From then on, Helen was clearly favored. When their father died in 1933, his will not only gave Helen a greater share of his estate and control of the newspaper but also promised that if May divorced Berryman, she could receive a larger annuity. The sisters fought in court and clashed again after Belle died, who also shorted May in favor of Helen. The hearing was noisy, but justice prevailed, splitting Belle's estate fifty-fifty and providing May more income. The estranged sisters let familial bonds wither. Helen forbade any mention of May in *The Post*'s pages, and May turned her attention to creating Belmar.

Belmar's western façade with the fountain now located in Hungarian Freedom Park. *Thomas J. Noel collection/Lakewood Heritage Center.*

With a budget topping $1 million, Benedict was given free rein. Guests drove down a long, tree-lined lane, encountering an elaborate iron gate trimmed in gilt and embellished with round medallions presenting the estate's name, with support columns topped by statues of Pan. Passing through, a statuary-bedecked circular drive brought guests to the door. Louis XVI would have admired the perfectly symmetrical neoclassical glazed terra-cotta façade inspired by the Petit Trianon at Versailles. The interior, while not quite as ornate as the French original, was stately nonetheless. Large, well-proportioned rooms boasted sparkling chandeliers illuminating priceless antiques, including a piano said to have been played by Frédéric Chopin, a chair sat in by Queen Victoria and a bed owned by Queen Marie Antoinette. A 1941 Burnham Hoyt–designed art gallery addition showcased works by old masters Holbein, Correggio and van Dyck, as well as pieces by newer artists including Corot, Modigliani and Picasso. West-facing windows looked out to an expansive lawn graced by a white marble fountain designed by Benedict. The rest of the 250-acre property, which spanned both sides of Wadsworth Boulevard, was used agriculturally, for raising cattle, sheep and chickens, and as a nature preserve, centered on the fifty-acre Kountze Lake.

By this time, Bonfils and Berryman were living apart, and she, despite church doctrine, divorced him in 1943. She later became involved with Charles Edwin Stanton, an architect and designer whom she had met at Central City Opera—she was a benefactor, and he was redecorating the adjacent Teller House. He was much younger, just forty-six to her seventy-three, when they married at Belmar in 1956, and until her 1962 death, she relied on him to manage her affairs. He lived on, selling the property east of Wadsworth to mall developer Gerri Von Frellick, who opened the Villa Italia center there in 1966. May would have undoubtedly appreciated the mall's collection of classical statuary reproductions, as she had filled her own home with similar baubles. In 1970, Stanton donated Belmar to the Denver Archdiocese, stipulating that it be used for religious purposes, but the diocese could not afford maintenance and sold it to a developer. Intending to replace the house and immediate grounds with an office complex, the developer allowed the archdiocese to open Belmar to the public for the first and last time, and in the fall of 1970, thousands came to gawk, marvel and mourn the impending loss of one of Colorado's finest mansions. Stanton, for his part, unsentimentally believed that once a house's builder dies, it becomes a "meaningless shell."

Today, the only remnants of Belmar on site are its ornate gate, a neoclassical boathouse and a wooden barn incorporated into the Lakewood Heritage Center. The marble fountain sparkles in Denver's Hungarian Freedom Park on Speer Boulevard at Emerson Street. The Belmar name lives on in the mixed-use development that replaced the outmoded Villa Italia. While some mourn the mall's passing, the bigger loss by far is May Bonfils's dream house.[5]

Bethell-Phipps Mansion

Impossible to imagine now, East Colfax Avenue from Sherman to York Streets was once a prestigious mansion-lined thoroughfare. One of the finest, at the southwestern corner of Colfax and Marion Street, was built for Captain William Decatur Bethell. A resident of Maury County southwest of Nashville and from a slaveholding family, Bethell joined the Confederate Twenty-Second Tennessee Infantry in 1861 as a twenty-one-year-old. He was wounded in the Hornet's Nest stage of the Battle of Shiloh in April 1862 and served out the war as a staff officer under Brigadier General Gideon Pillow, his wife Cynthia's relative. In 1882, he and his Pillow relations pooled funds to build Bethell House, a luxury hotel in Columbia, Tennessee. In 1891, he became president of the Taxing District, or de facto mayor, of disincorporated Memphis, Tennessee, but later that year, he left Memphis, came to Denver for his health and established the Southern Investment Company, headquartered in the Ernest and Cranmer Building (later relocating to the Mining Exchange Building). In September 1892, he bought struggling Manhattan Beach amusement park at Sloan's Lake, leasing it to a succession of management companies. How sound this investment was is unknown, but, beset by fires, drownings and other disasters, it likely broke even at best.

Bethell clearly had money, both inherited wealth and investment income, as he could engage young Theodore Davis Boal, who became a society favorite, to design a mansion in the Châteauesque style inspired by Loire Valley French Renaissance palaces. This aesthetic, with steeply pitched roofs, round towers, spires and other exotic elements, was highly fashionable in the 1890s; its best-known American example is Asheville, North Carolina's Biltmore, built contemporaneously with Bethell's mansion. Bethell's home was finished by mid-1893, when the Bethells held a ball honoring his cousin Louise Bethel Sneed, who met her future husband, Crawford Hill, at the event. It was built of white stone, and its red-tiled roof sheltered twenty-six rooms. Some were large, designed for lavish entertaining; the entry hall measured twenty-five feet square. Rooms were paneled in oak or mahogany and decorated with antique furniture and Persian carpets. An 1894 party hosted over seven hundred guests under electric chandeliers. The Bethells lived at 1154 East Colfax Avenue for seven years, departing in 1901. Bethell moved to California for its climate. He later returned to Denver, dying in 1906 at his daughter's home. Cynthia lived another fourteen years, residing at 850 Pearl Street.

In 1901, Lawrence Cowle Phipps, recently arrived from Pittsburgh, bought the home for $75,000 and spent a similar amount on renovations and redecorating. Phipps, nephew of industrialist Henry Phipps Jr., the second-largest shareholder in Carnegie Steel, had spent his adult working life there, rising to first vice president. In 1901, John Pierpont Morgan

The Bethell-Phipps Mansion, Colfax façade. *Denver Public Library, Western History Collection, H-582; photograph by Rose & Hopkins.*

purchased Carnegie and merged it with other companies to form United States Steel; the resulting financial payoff allowed Phipps to retire from business and move out west, retaining a significant stake in U.S. Steel. On the cusp of forty when he arrived, he chose Denver after a hunting trip introduced him to Colorado's charms. With Phipps came his second wife, Genevieve Chandler Phipps, and their two young daughters, Dorothy and Helen. Phipps's two older children by his deceased first wife remained back east, son Lawrence at Yale and daughter Emma at school in Dobbs Ferry, New York. Genevieve was fifteen years younger than Lawrence, whom she had married in 1897.

This immensely rich couple captivated society reporters, who chronicled every detail, true or not. Red-haired Genevieve was a "beautiful woman of the Titianesque type and with her personal attractions she possesses a cultivated mind and many accomplishments," one gushed. Her wardrobe and jewelry provided endless fascination. For a $100 daily fee, she retained designer Hubert De Rossi, who had decorated the Phippses' Pittsburgh mansion, Grand View, and had worked for "the Vanderbilts and other millionaires in the East." In January 1903, seven large paintings from the Phipps collection, insured for $35,000, hung at the R.L. Boutwell Art Gallery at 415 16th Street, where thousands viewed them prior to their installation in the mansion. Even for the girls, no expense was spared: Phipps's contractor built a children's playhouse of cement, twenty feet square and fifteen high. Phipps also erected a four-car garage.

The doting coverage of everything Phipps took a more sensational turn in June 1904, undoubtedly benefiting *The Denver Post*'s circulation; nearly every day between June and October, the Phipps name appeared in that gossipy broadsheet in connection with the biggest Denver divorce since Horace Tabor left Augusta for Baby Doe. Shocking news came that Lawrence had "kidnapped" their daughters from his wife's New York hotel suite to bring them home to Denver. Both sides retained counsel: friend Gerald Hughes for Lawrence, and for Genevieve, family friend Philander Chase Knox, who had served as attorney general for presidents William McKinley and Theodore Roosevelt. Locally, she hired former Denver mayor Platt Rogers. Lawrence, after engaging round-the-clock private security, filed for divorce on June 6, citing "incompatibility of temper and cruelty," claiming the condition had existed since the marriage's beginning. Genevieve instructed Rogers to file a writ of ejection against Lawrence: the Colfax mansion was in her name.

This would not do. Neither side relished publicity, but more importantly, the Phipps name was entwined with Carnegie and Morgan. The future of American capitalism was at stake, as revelations in court and in newspapers would show. Henry Phipps stepped in, strongly advising Lawrence to settle. Should the case proceed, the elder Phipps feared disaster, as not only did Genevieve's name appear on the titles of the Denver and Pittsburgh mansions but also on enough shares (valued at $10 million) of U.S. Steel that, should she decide to sell them to anyone not named Phipps, Carnegie or Morgan, it would deprive those oligarchs of control. Later in the summer, it emerged that she had been communicating with brokers representing John D. Rockefeller and George Jay Gould. She ultimately did not sell to them, but she knew her shares provided the strongest possible leverage with Lawrence. To prevent Morgan from reissuing the shares in Lawrence's name, she counter-sued for divorce in Pittsburgh, where she felt she could better control the outcome. She wanted custody of her daughters and the Pittsburgh house. Lawrence wanted custody too, but his uncle urged him to surrender to her demands.

After a summer filled with rumors—of reconciliation, of her plans to remarry, of Secret Service agents tracking Lawrence on Knox's orders, of offers and counteroffers—Judge Peter L. Palmer of Denver District Court granted divorce on September 14. Genevieve conveyed title to both mansions, along with all U.S. Steel bonds. With other bonds, Lawrence set up a trust fund, its interest to be paid to her as long as she remained unmarried. Should she remarry, the trust would dissolve, but she would receive bonds worth $250,000. Custody was split, each getting the girls for six-month periods and on alternate Christmases. Neither could remove the girls from the country without written permission of the other.

Why did it come to this? The answer seemingly appeared in courtroom testimony:

> *Judge Palmer: "State whether prior to the filing of this complaint, June 6, 1904, your wife for more than one year deserted you, failed to live with you as your wife and failed to perform her wifely duties toward you, and whether or not she threatened to break off all marital relations with you?"*
> *Lawrence Cowle Phipps: "Such is the fact. That is what she did."*

But what caused Lawrence to remove the girls from Genevieve and rush them back to Denver? Cessation of physical relations is not uncommon; many couples live this way without divorce. If *The Post* is to be believed, Genevieve was planning to leave Lawrence, take the girls to Europe and marry Andrew Hartupee McKee (who styled his name A. Hart McKee), son of a Pittsburgh glass manufacturer. They had known each other for years and were related by marriage. Several years earlier "at a Virginia resort there was a scene between Mr. and Mrs. Phipps and Hart McKee....This was followed a few months later by an encounter between the men in one of Pittsburg's most exclusive clubs...where the combatants came to blows." The day before the "kidnapping," a personal advertisement appeared in a New York newspaper: "Hart—Meet me at the Manhattan, as usual. Monday at noon; important. 'DIMPLES.'" This was Genevieve's nickname. Lawrence, tipped off by the family's governess and nurse, hired detectives and devised a plan for these servants to take the girls out for an "airing," during which he would arrive and take custody.

After the divorce, *The Post* continued to speculate on Genevieve's future. Rumors again arose of McKee's intention to marry her, but he remained married to Lydia Sutton McKee, who refused to grant his "freedom." Genevieve took pains to deny rumors: "The statement recently made that I am about to marry A. Hart McKee is absolutely without foundation. The many exaggerated statements which have appeared in the press during the last few months have caused me great sorrow and now that my marital differences with my husband have been adjusted to his and my satisfaction, I sincerely hope that we may be spared further publicity."

McKee then sailed to Europe with Cornelia Baxter Tevis. This "attractive young widow" of California millionaire Hugh Tevis, who had died on his honeymoon, was daughter to former Wyoming governor George White Baxter, a millionaire cattle rancher living in Denver. Circulating in high society, Cornelia had been engaged to Gerald Hughes. For the 1900 Festival of Mountain and Plain, she had reigned as "Queen of the Silver Serpent." Genevieve had introduced her to McKee, who, despite his promises and nearly $100,000 he provided Genevieve during her divorce from Lawrence, became infatuated and quietly began making plans with Cornelia. Their departure surely shocked Genevieve—now she was divorced and bereft of her paramour. After returning from Europe, McKee and Tevis married in Philadelphia. Then came the McKee divorce court transcript from Pittsburgh, printed in full in the *Rocky Mountain News*, with Lydia McKee testifying that her husband had physically and emotionally abused her since their 1892 wedding. Genevieve never revealed how this revelation affected her, but had she married McKee, she might have been unhappy. Instead, she remained in Denver for some time to be near her daughters. Lawrence helped her repay her financial debt to McKee.

Lawrence Phipps remained a major U.S. Steel stockholder, but he also invested in Colorado concerns, including the Denver and Salt Lake Railroad. He became a major Colorado philanthropist. Even during the torrid summer of 1904, as divorce news filled newspaper columns, he oversaw completion of the Agnes Memorial Sanitarium, named for his mother, near East 6th Avenue and Quebec Street. He donated to the Denver Zoo, Children's Hospital and Denver Museum of Natural History, where he paid for a large lecture auditorium, now the museum's IMAX theater. A few years after his divorce, he married Margaret Rogers, daughter of Platt Rogers. Twenty-seven years his junior, and younger than his two eldest children, she bore him his fifth and sixth offspring, Allen Rogers Phipps (1912) and Gerald Hughes Phipps (1915), whose earliest memories would have been of the mansion on Colfax Avenue. In 1918, Colorado voters elected the Republican Phipps to the U.S. Senate, where he served until 1931.

By this time, Colfax's former grandeur had disappeared, with mansions replaced by apartments and commercial buildings. Even in 1902, his first year living in the former Bethell mansion, Phipps pressured John S. Flower, president of the Denver Real Estate Exchange, not to build a one-story retail building across Colfax (instead, Flower built in 1905 an elegant three-story apartment building with ground-floor shops, extant today). Few grand houses remained in 1929, their front yards replaced by tacked-on retail storefronts; it was time to leave. In 1932, Margaret and Lawrence, after a few years renting 161 Race Street, occupied their newly constructed Belcaro, a 33,123-square-foot, fifty-four-room mansion in a neighborhood Phipps himself developed. Phipps lived to his ninety-fifth year, dying in 1958; Margaret died in 1968. By this time, Phipps's first Denver home was gone, demolished in the 1950s for an ugly motor hotel that, as of this writing, is itself slated for redevelopment.[6]

Charles Boettcher II Mansion

When Charles Boettcher II married Anna Lou Pigott of Helena, Montana, in 1926, his father, Claude Kedzie Boettcher, commissioned Harry James Manning to design a home for the newlyweds. With its half-timbering, leaded diamond-pane windows, octagonal weathervane-topped stair tower, rustic shingled roof and other faux-medieval details, Les Trois Tours at 777 Washington Street, on the southwest corner with 8th Avenue, radiated storybook charm. Yet what occurred here would not be the stuff of children's literature but of popular detective magazines. The drama of Charles's 1933 kidnapping captured the nation's attention when the Federal Bureau of Investigation, directed by J. Edgar Hoover, named Boettcher's kidnapper Public Enemy No. 1 until his capture.

By 1926, the Boettcher name carried great weight in Colorado. Charles II was the third generation of a dynasty that his German immigrant grandfather Charles had founded when he arrived in Colorado in 1871. From his beginning as a hardware merchant, he built a business empire that encompassed Great Western Sugar, Ideal Cement, banking interests and other concerns. Son Claude's brokerage firm, Boettcher, Newton & Company, ruled 17th Street, "Wall Street of the Rockies," from offices in the Boston Building, financing such mega-projects as the Moffat Tunnel under the Continental Divide. The Boettchers also owned Denver's finest hotel, The Brown Palace, where the elder Charles spent his last years. Claude and his second wife, Edna, living just down 8th Avenue from Charles II in a 1908 mansion built for Alice Cheesman, dominated Denver society; today, their home is the Governor's Residence at Boettcher Mansion. Charles II was born in 1901; when he married Anna Lou, he was twenty-four and recently graduated from Yale. Shortly after the house's 1927 completion, the young couple hosted a combination housewarming and first-anniversary dinner party for fifty guests.

The Charles Boettcher II Mansion, Washington Street façade, 1948. *Denver Public Library, Western History Collection, X-26284; photograph by Orin A. Sealy.*

Journalists were extraordinarily busy in early 1933. Nationally, the repeal of Prohibition was coming. The banking system was verging on collapse. On February 15, Giuseppe Zangara attempted to kill President-elect Franklin Delano Roosevelt, mortally wounding Chicago mayor Anton Cermak. Locally, early 1933 witnessed banks shutting down and the closure of a department store popular with the well-to-do, A.T. Lewis & Son; it also saw the bloody gangland slaying of North Denver bootlegger Joe Roma. The legislature was debating a bill that would make kidnapping—a crime that increasingly dominated the national imagination after 1932's abduction and murder of Charles Augustus Lindbergh Jr., twenty-month-old son of the famous aviator (and Boettcher family friend)—a capital offense. The press capitalized on this "epidemic," creating mass hysteria far out of proportion to the actual number of kidnappings committed. In Denver, no newspaper was better at creating a sensation than *The Denver Post*. The Boettcher kidnapping would dominate its pages for weeks, nearly crowding out Roosevelt.

On Sunday evening, February 12, Charles and Anna Lou, after visiting friends and buying some take-out chili to bring home, returned

The Charles Boettcher II Mansion, 8th Avenue façade, showing the driveway where the kidnapping occurred, 1933. *Author's collection.*

after dark. Pulling off 8th Avenue into the driveway, Charles got out to open the garage door when two men appeared. They forced Boettcher into another car and handed a ransom note to Anna Lou, demanding $60,000 for his safe return. It was immediately a national story; under the (correct) assumption that Boettcher was being held in another state, the FBI involved itself, empowered by the 1932 "Lindbergh Law," which made interstate kidnapping a federal offense. Governor Edwin C. Johnson rallied Coloradans to join the search for Boettcher; the American Legion and other organizations got involved. Socialites bought guns for self-protection. Both 8th Avenue mansions became "armed camps," with Denver police providing security from potential threats and hordes of inquisitive Denverites passing slowly by hoping for a glimpse of anyone named Boettcher. Claude assumed control, with Anna Lou, pregnant with her second child, keeping out of sight other than pleading with legislators to postpone the kidnapping bill lest its passage endanger her husband's life. She also tended their first child, likewise named Anna Lou, who wondered why her daddy did not return from his trip; journalists likened the distraught wife to Anne Morrow Lindbergh. Claude shut out law enforcement, negotiating directly with the kidnappers through letters and two intermediaries, his business partner James Quigg Newton (father of a later Denver mayor) and the dean of St. John's Episcopal Church, Benjamin D. Dagwell. He told journalists, "Obviously, the police, the press, myself and family are each actuated by different motives—the police primarily to apprehend the culprits, the press to print all the news, myself and family to accomplish the safe return of my son."

The plot's mastermind who had handed Anna Lou the ransom note was Verne Sankey, described by her as "about forty-two years old," five-foot-seven, weighing between 150 and 160 pounds, with "peculiar round eyes"; collaborator Gordon Alcorn, in his late twenties, forced Boettcher into his Ford V-8, binding his eyes with adhesive tape. The two culprits had met when both worked for a Canadian railroad; prior to taking up crime, Sankey had worked legitimate jobs, but by the time of the Boettcher kidnapping, he had kidnapped, robbed and bootlegged for years, with liquor clients among Boettcher's "17th Street crowd." Rapidly exiting Denver, they sped north to Sankey's South Dakota turkey farm, an isolated spot on the Crow Creek Reservation eighteen hours from Denver, with Boettcher blindfolded the entire time. Arriving at the farmhouse, the tape came off, but he was warned not to look at his captors. Also present was farm caretaker Arthur Youngberg, another railroad alum who guarded Boettcher while Sankey returned to Denver to negotiate. His Denver headquarters were at 2292 South Emerson Street, where fellow conspirator Carl W. Pearce, a Denver insurance salesman, typed the letters to Claude. Also concerned were Sankey's wife, Fern, who cooked Charles's meals, and her sister Alvina Ruth Kohler, who was involved with Pearce.

Sankey's negotiations paid off; Claude agreed to their terms, following instructions to drop the cash into a dry creek bed north of Denver. Just after midnight on March 1, his captors taped Charles's eyes and bundled him back into the car to return him to Denver, arriving after nightfall. They dropped him off on Gaylord Street near 34th Avenue (now Bruce Randolph Avenue); after removing the tape, he made his way to nearby Reed's Drug Store at 34th and York Street, where he telephoned his father and ordered a chocolate milkshake while waiting to be picked up. Druggist Frank Reed had no idea that this disheveled man in a dirty suit was the most talked-about kidnap victim since the Lindbergh baby, but he figured it out when reporters showed up. Word quickly spread, and by the time Boettcher reached home, he had to be secreted into a different house on

Living room of the Charles Boettcher II Mansion, 1948. *Denver Public Library, Western History Collection, X-26291; photograph by Orin A. Sealy.*

the block and then brought up the alley to the back door to avoid curiosity seekers blocking 8th Avenue and Washington Street.

Although police kept watch over the money drop and pursued Sankey to Greeley, he eluded them, remaining at large until January 31, 1934, when the FBI caught him in a Chicago barbershop, awaiting a shave, his face under a hot towel. The press was hot for information and brimming with theories.

Several reporters tried tying him to the Lindbergh kidnapping. He bristled, "I am a man. I'd kidnap another man. I'd never touch a baby." He was transferred to Sioux Falls, South Dakota, for trial. Unwilling to face prison, he managed to bind two neckties together into a noose and died in his cell eight days after his capture. Alcorn, Pearce and Youngberg were convicted and sent to Leavenworth. The oddly cheerful Alcorn, who had also been arrested in Chicago, told deputies that he "had a swell time with my share of the ransom. I bet I made all the nightclubs in Chicago. The money's all gone now, every cent of it, and I'm ready to take the consequences. I never was cut out for this kidnapping racket anyhow." Charles Boettcher aided investigators every way he could, even returning to Sankey's ranch with G-men to verify that it was his kidnappers' lair. After a rest, he returned to the brokerage, promoted Colorado aviation (flying was his passion) and lived the life of a Boettcher, making frequent ocean voyages with Anna Lou to their vacation home, built in 1935 on Kailua Beach on Oahu. In 1941 Anna Lou, after a long illness, committed suicide in the Denver house; Charles remarried a few years later to widow Mae Scott Foster. In 1949, he was named head of the Colorado Civil Air Patrol.

Boettcher sold the Washington Street home for $50,000 in 1952 to a Colorado Springs resident who rented it out. In 1956, Denver police, tipped off to an illegal gambling operation, raided the mansion, and it sat empty. In 1958, a developer bought it to demolish for an apartment house, but plans fell through. By 1962, the city had deemed the derelict structure a public nuisance, calling for its demolition. A few preservation-minded citizens rallied to prevent this fate, ironically within a week of Charles Boettcher II's death at the age of sixty-one, but the house was flattened shortly thereafter. The lot sat empty for a decade; in 1973, construction began on Governor's Park, a high-rise condominium that bears the same address, 777, as the lost Boettcher storybook house.[7]

BRINTON TERRACE

That Brinton Terrace, in life's vortex caught,
Must fall into our dreams of memory things.
—*Jean Milne Gower, "Old Brinton Terrace," 1947*

On the northwest corner of 18th Avenue and Lincoln Street is an asphalt-paved lot tucked behind Trinity Methodist Church. Few now realize that this corner once represented Denver's version of Greenwich Village, an apartment building (or terrace) filled with what were then called Bohemians: journalists, painters, sculptors, photographers, architects, musicians, conductors, singers, anyone enjoying *la vie Bohème*. The three-story building presented a picturesque appearance, divided into three sections, with roof gable-ends facing 18th Avenue and, in the central section, two tall chimneys. Visitors climbed stairways to first-floor entries, each rising over belowground areas with basement entries. Ground- and third-floor windows were arched. Two upper floors, half-timbered, almost Tudor in style but still within the realm of the then-prevailing Queen Anne mode, topped the red brick (later painted white) first floor; the overall effect was perceived as "English." Some have credited Frederick Junius Sterner with the design, although at the time of its construction, he was just twenty years old, working as a draftsman for Frank E. Edbrooke, and would not form his partnership with Ernest Phillip Varian until two years later. Some have also credited Irish aesthete Oscar Wilde with opining that "Brinton Terrace is the only artistic building in Denver," although his Denver sojourn occurred in April 1882, two months prior to the start of Brinton Terrace's construction. Perhaps someone showed him an architectural rendering.

William Shaw Ward, builder of Brinton Terrace, was a man of many interests and abilities. Born in Madurai, Madras, India, to missionary parents, he served in the U.S. Navy during the Civil War and then obtained a metallurgy degree from Columbia; attracted to Colorado's silver boom, he became manager and partial owner of Leadville's Morning Star and Evening Star mines on Carbonate Hill, profits from which likely funded construction of Brinton Terrace. Additional financing may have come from Ulysses S. Grant or his family, as Ward's brother Ferdinand was the former president's business partner, and when Grant visited Colorado in 1880, Ward hosted him. Ward must have envisioned not only that Denver would grow denser—at the time, Henry C. Brown's cows still grazed nearby and Brinton Terrace residents enjoyed a clear line of sight to Augusta Tabor's mansion one block south—but that it would also need housing for wealthy people who did not want a house surrounded by a yard. As initially configured, Brinton Terrace contained six ten-room apartments, including servants' quarters below the eaves, and its first tenants came from the ranks of what was then called "respectable" society. Addresses on East 18th Avenue were 23, 25, 27, 31, 33 and 35 (with 29 and 37 subdivided later, along with 1803 and 1807 Lincoln). Ward named the complex for his brother-in-law Dr. John Brinton, president of the College of Physicians and Surgeons at the University of Pennsylvania.

Brinton Terrace as viewed from the alley east toward Lincoln Street, 1919. *Denver Public Library, Western History Collection, X-22369.*

Soon enough, Brown's cattle gave way to Trinity Methodist Church across the alley, the Hotel Metropole (later Cosmopolitan) and Broadway Theatre across 18th and The Brown Palace Hotel across Broadway.

Ward and his wife, Eliza Jane, lived in Brinton Terrace for some years. Joining them there was *Denver Tribune* president Ottomar H. Rothacker. It was he who hired journalist/poet Eugene Field as the paper's managing editor, and Field was a frequent guest at Rothacker's home, as were humorist Bill Nye and Frederick J.V. Skiff, then the *Tribune*'s treasurer but later director of the 1893 World's Columbian Exposition in Chicago and involved with later world's fairs in Paris and Louisiana. It may have been this connection that led to Ward's selection as curator of Colorado's mining exhibits at those fairs. The Wards had four children while living at Brinton Terrace and moved freely in Denver's social and artistic circles, with William serving as the first president of the Denver Art League, formed in 1892. In 1905, the new Colorado Museum of Natural History named him its first director of minerals, as well as of art and archaeology. He served the museum until 1914 and died in 1917.

Other early residents were similarly professional, academic or elite in other ways. Notable was Dr. Henry M. Sewall, who lived in number 23 in the 1890s. Earlier, Sewall had served as the first president of the University of Colorado and founder of its medical school and was then one of Colorado's most prestigious physicians, with a national reputation. Dr. Samuel A. Fisk, like Sewall a tuberculosis specialist, lived here simultaneously, as did Dr. Mary H. Barker Bates. Judge Gilbert Reed of the Colorado Court of Appeals had rooms here, as did several bankers and capitalists.

Everything changed in 1906 and 1907. Ward no longer owned the building, having sold it in 1897 to Julia Merritt. In 1906, Margaret S. Van Waganen, "a protégé of Miss Anne Evans" (a towering figure in Denver's arts history, having helped found both the Denver Art Museum and the Central City Opera House Association), took over management, intending to assemble artists "under one roof where they might unite in a common cause and derive inspiration from one another." Existing tenants' leases were terminated, and soon workmen began removing walls, installing skylights and creating commercial spaces on the street floor. Two brothers, R.L. and Cyrus Boutwell, opened Boutwell's Art Store, "full of lovely gifts and household things, mirrors and candlesticks and quaint chairs and mahogany tables and old prints," in number 23, relocating from 16th Street. Next door, Denver's first art gallery, the Brinton Studio House, occupied number 25, with the Gotham Shop, an antique emporium, in number 27.

A fine book dealer occupied number 31, and an Oriental rug merchant took number 35. In between, number 33 housed the atelier of architects Maurice Biscoe and Henry Harwood Hewitt, designers of numerous fine mansions. Another tenant was the Tea Cup Inn, "broad low rooms in a prevailing note of blue, with Japanese iris stenciled upon the walls and curtains and upon the runners which decorate the dark oak tables," where Belle Herzinger and Alice Fisher served "delicious tea, delectable salads and queer cakes," leading Denver to become, "thru the influence of this sociable tearoom, very English in its taste for afternoon tea-drinking." The Boutwell brothers appear to have curated the Brinton Studio House; among its early exhibitions was a one-man show by George Elbert Burr, a nationally recognized etcher who occupied rooms upstairs for two years (his later home at 1325 Logan Street became the Denver Women's Press Club). In 1908, tenants launched a quarterly art magazine.

Upstairs spaces became smaller apartments or day studios; demand was high and vacancies rare. Charles Waldo Love, painter of early diorama backgrounds at the natural history museum, leased an apartment in 1909. Living here also in this period was Allen Tupper True, a Manual High School alum recently graduated from Washington, D.C.'s Corcoran School of Art and Wilmington, Delaware's Howard Pyle School. During his Brinton Terrace period True painted mostly illustrations for books and magazines, along with framed pieces, including one for Anne Evans; later, he would gain renown as a muralist, his works gracing landmarks in Denver and other places. Another muralist and sculptor, Dudley Carpenter, lived here with his wife, Margaret, who specialized in stained glass. Illustrating Margaret Van Waganen's concept of artistic collaboration between tenants, Biscoe designed the Carnegie-funded Dickinson branch library at 1550 Hooker Street, opened in 1913 with medallions of "distinguished literary men" by Carpenter and murals of frontier life by True. Not all Brinton Terrace artists were men; Alice Best and Helen Dougall created jewelry; Jane Porter Robinson painted portraits and landscapes; and photographers Wilma Wallace and Anne Dailey also created portraits.

Another female tenant, Sarah Lacy, kept a drama studio upstairs in number 25, where she also taught conversation and deportment. She hosted events for the Denver Women's Press Club and the Denver Drama League, the latter group enjoying Brinton Terrace's proximity to the Broadway Theatre, which frequently hosted traveling New York productions. In 1912, Lacy held a reception for actress Margaret Illington, who was then performing at the Broadway; among the guests were Louise Sneed Hill, Sarah Platt Decker and other social lights. A very different sort of woman appeared at Brinton Terrace in 1912, one better remembered than Illington: Emma Goldman, accompanied by her lover, Dr. Ben Reitman. The famous anarchist and free love advocate spoke not to fellow travelers but instead to the cream of Denver society; it was a "sweetly pretty anarchistic party," according to *Rocky Mountain News* social columnist Alice Rohe, but also "deadly dull" due to the presence of the pompous Reitman. Rohe did not name names, other than "many, many prominent people," but one extraordinary guest was named: William Dudley "Big Bill" Haywood, the "Lincoln of Labor" whose cremains reside in the Kremlin Wall. Years earlier, Haywood had been kidnapped from Denver to face trial for the 1905 assassination of Idaho governor Frank Steunenberg (he was defended by Clarence Darrow, who secured his acquittal).

Then there were the Gowers, Dr. John H.; his wife, Jean; and their daughter, Gwendoline, artists all, who from 1917 lived in an atmosphere that "smack[ed] of the eighteenth century" in number 23. The English Dr. Gower had become famous at eleven years old when Queen Victoria appointed him organist of the Princess Royal Chapel at Windsor, and by the time he lived in Brinton Terrace, he was considered one of the world's top organists. Mayor Robert W. Speer, when planning for the Municipal Organ in the Municipal Auditorium, worked closely with Gower. Jean Gower painted, but her true calling was poetry, and she penned a poetry column for the *Rocky Mountain News*; number 23 came to be called "Poet's Corner."

Dr. Gower was not Brinton Terrace's only musician; by the time of his residency, the building was attracting many performing artists. One was Dr. Wilberforce J. Whiteman, choral director of Trinity Methodist, head of music for Denver Public Schools and father of Paul Whiteman, the "King of Jazz," one of America's most popular bandleaders in the interwar period (Paul never lived in Brinton Terrace but certainly visited). Horace Elder Tureman occupied a studio, composing, teaching music and conducting the Elitch Gardens Orchestra; he later became the Denver Symphony Orchestra's first conductor. Florence Taussig established her Piano School in number 35. Other musicians and singers, well known to Denver audiences, also lived here, along with vocal coaches and music instructors; on warm summer afternoons, with windows open, the air would have been filled with a cacophony of sounds.

Brinton Terrace was also home to two organized schools of the arts. The first was the Western Institute of Music and Dramatic Art, established by Frederick Schweikher in number 29. In 1914, he moved the school to the

View of downtown from El Jebel Temple, showing Brinton Terrace in the foreground, 1910. *Denver Public Library, Western History Collection, MCC-1268; photograph by Louis Charles McClure.*

top floor of the Denham Theater Building downtown, then to Wolfe Hall; he also headed the University of Denver's College of Music. In 1920, John Campbell Cory opened the Denver Academy of Fine and Applied Arts in number 35, offering classes in painting, commercial art, illustration, cartooning, fashion drawing, portraiture, interior design and other subjects. Its star faculty member was John Edward Thompson, who also lived in Brinton Terrace. Thompson introduced modern art to Colorado, having spent his early adulthood studying in Amsterdam and Paris, where he was influenced by Cézanne and the Fauves and knew Gertrude Stein. In 1919, having relocated to Colorado, he organized a show for the Denver Art Association that caused such controversy with its radical new art that it was dubbed "Denver's Armory Show," after the similarly shocking 1913 New York spectacle. Joining him on the faculty were luminaries Laura Gilpin, Paul St. Gaudens, Arnold Rönnebeck, Anne Van Briggle Ritter, David Spivak, Robert Garrison, Henry McCarter and Robert Graham. Garrison, a student of Mount Rushmore sculptor Gutzon Borglum, collaborated with Denver architects; his work includes the Sea Lion Fountain at the Voorhees Memorial in Civic Center and many gargoyles and other sculptures at South High School.

In the 1920s and later, Brinton Terrace became a center for photography. The Wiswall brothers (Bruce and Wilbur), Robert A. Officer and Charles Mace all had studios. P.T. Blackburn, then a scenic artist for the Denham Theater, lived at 1803 Lincoln; in 1928, he threw a birthday party in his apartment for one of the Denham Players, Gale Gordon, who later worked with Lucille Ball. In the 1930s and 1940s, milliner Cornelius Kittredge, creator of *haute couture* hats popular with society women (and the son of Charles Marble Kittredge), lived in number 29. In 1942, Dutch conductor and pianist Antonia Louisa Brico moved into Brinton Terrace as the last of its famous tenants. Brico had earlier become the first woman to conduct the New York Philharmonic; in Denver, she established a Bach Society and conducted the Denver Businessmen's Orchestra, later the Brico Symphony. She also taught conducting and piano; singer Judy Collins, who grew up in Denver, was her most famous piano student.

There was certainly some self-consciousness in Brinton Terrace's pretentions to Bohemia, but the artistry represented by its residents was real, as was the fellowship. "Drop in to any of the studios in Brinton Terrace today," *The Post*'s Frances Wayne wrote in 1919, "and one is guaranteed a lung full of Bohemian—whatever that may be—air along with fine music, clever talk, poetry, criticism, cigarettes, etc." It lasted for several decades, with Denver changing around it, until it finally succumbed in 1956, victim of Denver's collective postwar sense of inferiority. Shortsighted property owners had no use for Brinton Terrace. In a more civilized city, it would surely still stand, its walls crowded with plaques commemorating artists who once called it home.[8]

Fletcher Mansion

In a parking lot on the southwest corner of 16th Avenue and Grant Street stands a mysterious building. Built of rusticated red sandstone, it follows no architectural logic. Two stories high, its entry seems to be through an arched doorway at the base of a round tower topped by a conical roof, but at its southern end it is attached to a modern building with a simple glass door. Tall windows, filled in with glass block, span two floors and run for most of the façade's length. The north wall is blank. This peculiar building is all that remains of a much larger structure, an extravagant mansion built for real estate speculator Donald George Fletcher, who succeeded spectacularly until the Panic of 1893 left him in dire straits. His home, which faced banker Charles B. Kountze's massive domicile across 16th Avenue, set him back $150,000 for building and land. It was fully ten lots on Grant, then Denver's most expensive residential street, dubbed "Millionaire's Row." At the time, Fletcher was one of Denver's wealthiest men, with a fortune estimated at ten times the mansion's cost.

Canadian by birth, thirty-year-old Fletcher arrived in Colorado in 1879, journeying to Manitou Springs for his health. An ordained minister, in 1881 he became pastor of a Boulder Congregational church. As a sideline, he dabbled in real estate, found quick success and forsook the cloth in 1882 to embark on a meteoric career. He bought and sold thousands of lots in rapidly developing east Denver, platted Fletcher's West Side Subdivision between the South Platte River and today's Federal Boulevard and established subdivisions in Pueblo, where he also served as Colorado Mineral Palace president. Perhaps his best-known development was a suburb several miles east of Denver: Fletcher, Colorado, incorporated in 1891, bearing his name. To ensure its success, Fletcher and partners bought a streetcar company that ran out East Colfax Avenue, extending it to their town. It struggled; in 1907, with its namesake no longer a Coloradan and blamed for its financial woes, citizens voted to rename it Aurora. Fletcher was also active in community organizations, serving as president of the Denver Chamber of Commerce and the Denver Real Estate Exchange. In 1888, congregants of Central Presbyterian Church relied on Fletcher to procure suitable real estate; he facilitated the purchase of lots at 17th Avenue and Sherman Street where their landmark church stands today. In 1890, he was the first president of Fairmount Cemetery Association. For West Side High School, he established the Donald Fletcher Medal, an annual oratory prize with gold and silver versions; if a boy won gold, then the best girl won silver, and vice versa.

Fletcher was not shy about advertising his success. By the late 1880s, it was time for his family—wife Julia, son John and daughters Florence and Anne—to occupy a house befitting his status. After buying lots on Grant at 16th, he commissioned Chicago architect Henry Ives Cobb to design a fitting monument. Cobb was used to millionaires; Chicago's Potter Palmer had commissioned him for his massive Gold Coast mansion. After two years of construction, Fletcher's family took up residence at 1575 Grant in 1891, just before Thanksgiving. Three months later, on February 23, 1892, the

The Donald Fletcher Mansion, circa 1893. *History Colorado, 20100081; photograph by William Henry Jackson.*

mansion made its social debut, with over seven hundred invitations mailed to Denver's upper crust. Although it was snowing, scores of carriages made their way up the home's driveway, with guests entering from the *porte-cochère* on the south side or from the massive front door facing Grant. Inside, guests encountered masses of flowers in every room. Floors were of white oak, with fine rugs preventing sound from echoing off high ceilings; the library was floored in marble. In addition to the usual main-floor rooms and second-floor bedrooms (of which there were eight and four baths), visitors encountered a "fine art gallery, great sun-parlors, and Roman baths that are probably the most pretentious in the West." The third floor housed servants' quarters, along with a large ballroom. In the basement, the house boasted a bowling alley and swimming pool. At the property's southern end, a separate stone building in the same style served as an elaborate barn.

Fletcher did not enjoy the house for long, occupying it for about the same amount of time as it took to build. The Panic of 1893 left him owning hundreds of lots that nobody wanted and owing vast sums to lenders. His "fortune melted with the rapidity of a cake of ice on a torrid summer's day," per a later account, and despite his insistence that "most of my indebtedness...matures in 1895, 1896 and 1897 [and] I am able, in the meantime, to keep up the interest...I am not anxious or worried," he was apprehensive. He told a reporter, "I was talking with my family two evenings ago, and they said in one voice that they could be as happy and contented in six rooms as in this house. I expect to live in this house twenty years but I should not grieve if I could not live in it twenty months." After Union National Bank foreclosed, he moved to a five-room cottage nearby on 17th Avenue and then to 1236 Ogden Street. In 1896, he attempted to restart his career in booming Cripple Creek, then enjoying its gold rush; when that town burned twice in four days, he chaired the relief committee. Finding no luck promoting real estate there, he moved to New York City, where in 1899 he filed for bankruptcy. Emerging from that, he relocated to Seattle. There he managed to rebuild some of his fortune and was soon as big of a Seattle booster as he had been for Denver, Pueblo and Fletcher. Yet he still loved the city of his first fortune. In a 1907 visit, he proclaimed that Denver should become the capital of the United States. "The air in Denver is a tonic," he said. "It is champagne and all other places are beer. The intellect is quickened and a spirit of optimism is created. Men and women are made well and are kept in good health by the climate. Everybody who has more than a scant living should spend part of their time in Colorado every year, as it will add 10 per cent to their lives." Fletcher continued making Denver trips to sell his remaining real estate, staying at the economical American House on Blake Street rather than pricier hotels. He died in San Leandro, California, in 1929; his ashes reside in an Oakland mausoleum.

Fletcher's lender, Union National Bank, itself failed, and its appointed receiver had to get 1575 Grant off its books. No one was buying, so the receiver sought renters, finding General Elwell Stephen Otis, commander of the U.S. Army's Department of Colorado. He lived in it for a year or two before leaving to fight in the Philippines during the Spanish-American War. Realtors Bennett and Myers took over after he departed, advertising the "greatest bargain in Denver," priced far below what Fletcher had spent to build it. There were no takers until 1899, when cattle baron John Wallace Springer paid $50,000 cash for it as a home for himself and summer home for his father-in-law, Colonel William Edgar Hughes, another wealthy cattle baron with vast holdings in Texas and Montana. Hughes soon relocated permanently to the mansion, removing his Continental Land and Cattle Company headquarters from Dallas to the Boston Building on 17th Street. In 1899, Hughes received a delegation from German emperor Kaiser Wilhelm II. The embassy in Washington had heard of Hughes's fine, strong horses and sent a representative to purchase several hundred animals for the German army. Hughes gained a reputation for owning the finest horses and most elegant carriages in Denver; "his livery was irreproachable," per one account, inspiring other members of Denver's upper crust to upgrade their own.

In 1906, Springer and Hughes sold the mansion for $100,000 to Frank J. Hearne, president of the Colorado Fuel and Iron Company (CF&I), the Pueblo steel mill and coal mining concern. Since his 1903 appointment to that post by CF&I's new owners, John D. Rockefeller and George Jay Gould, Hearne and his wife had made Denver, rather than Pueblo, their home, first renting a mansion on Sherman Street and then living at The Brown Palace temporarily while contractors remodeled the Fletcher Mansion. It was likely Hearne who ordered construction of the wing connecting the barn with the house, although as originally constructed, it had a red sandstone ground floor with a sloping roof above, pierced by several dormers. Hearne and his wife collected art and antiques, filling the house with "rare statuary, fine old masterpieces, furniture marvelously carved and speaking of the monasteries of the old world, where it was discovered by the Hearnes in their wanderings abroad; brasses from an old cathedral in Mexico, New England mahogany in colonial design" and other *objets d'art*. An adoring newspaper account, ignoring Hearne's brutal treatment of CF&I's miners in a 1903–04 strike, waxed poetic, describing him as the "Bismarck type of man," implying both physical strength and "rare courage." Yet these qualities did not save him when he was felled by "the grip," declining steadily in his Brown suite, attended by the hotel's doctor and his personal physician. He passed before he ever resided in the Fletcher Mansion. His wife and son William lived in it briefly before relocating to Kansas City in 1909, emptying it of its treasures, which filled two rail cars.

The Hearne estate owned the house for another decade; in 1918, it was considered for an overflow hospital during the influenza pandemic, although it is unclear if it was used. It also hosted the Tallyho Dance Academy, operated by Susanne Perry. In 1919, the Knights of Columbus Council 539, a Roman Catholic fraternal service order, paid $52,500 for the property, relocating their clubhouse from 14th Street and Glenarm Place. The neighborhood had changed greatly, its original complement of millionaires either dead or relocated to plusher palaces. The Kountze Mansion became a rooming house. The Knights modified the south wing in 1928, creating a meeting hall by removing the roof and dormers and doubling its height. The organization took good care of the house that Fletcher built, briefly turning it over to the USO during World War II. In 1948, *Denver Post* editor

The Donald Fletcher Mansion with its south wing (*left*), 1948. *Denver Public Library, Western History Collection, Z-269; photograph by Orin A. Sealy.*

Palmer Hoyt assigned Edith Eudora Kohl to write articles on Denver's old mansions, with photography by Orin A. Sealy. His photographs reveal a well-preserved remnant of Denver's gilded age. Yet in 1961, the house came down for a projected office building facing the new Capitol Life tower on the former Kountze property. It was not entirely demolished; the south wing was saved and attached to a new Knights of Columbus building bearing the address 1555 Grant. The loss of the Fletcher Mansion proved futile: the projected office tower never got built, and more than six decades later the land occupied by the main house functions as parking.[9]

HOYT HOUSE

Like the neighboring Anderson House, the Hoyt House was a casualty of the twenty-first-century development mania that has destroyed most of Jefferson Park's charm. Located at 2839 West 23rd Avenue, this was an eclectic, 1888–89 two-story Queen Anne with most of its historic character intact. Its original owners, Wallace A. and Lydia Tompkins Hoyt, were parents of two prominent Denver architects, Merrill H. and Burnham F. Hoyt. The boys

The Hoyt House, 2016. *Wikimedia Commons, photograph by Denverjoan.*

grew up here, walking to nearby Boulevard School and North High School, and as adults they often returned until their widowed mother sold it.

Merrill became an architect in 1899, working in William E. Fisher's office and then founding his own firm in 1915. Six years younger, Burnham followed a similar path initially, working in Franklin E. Kidder and T. Robert Wieger's practice, but with Merrill's encouragement, he applied to New York's Beaux-Arts Institute, where he shined; he then worked for New York architects George B. Post and Bertram Goodhue. In 1919, after two years of army service, he returned to Denver to join Merrill in partnership. The Hoyts won several notable commissions, including the Park Hill Branch Library, Lake Junior High School and St. Martin's Chapel at St. John's Cathedral. Merrill served as Rocky Mountain director for the Architects' Small House Service Bureau, creating middle-class housing solutions. In 1926, John D. Rockefeller Jr. asked Burnham to design the interior of Riverside Church, and Hoyt remained in New York, assuming the deanship of New York University's School of Architecture. Merrill died in 1933. When Burnham returned to Denver three years later, he had mastered the new International style. During this mature period, he designed lauded buildings for the Boettcher School for Crippled Children and the Albany Hotel and several iconic Modernist residences. Most famously, he designed Red Rocks Amphitheatre, named by the Museum of Modern Art as one of fifty outstanding architectural works of the 1940s. His final completed work was the four-story Denver Public Library facing Civic Center across 14th Avenue. By the time of his 1960 death, he was known as "Colorado's foremost mid-20th-century architect," prominent enough to warrant a *New York Times* obituary.

This mattered little to the homeowner, who saw developer's dollars funding a retirement. In 2016, when the owner applied for a certificate of non-historic status, city councilman Rafael Espinoza filed with the DLPC for historic designation. Historic Denver, Inc. got involved, seeking a preservation solution that would yield the same financial benefit to the owner. The DLPC hearing became contentious, with the owner's friends and neighbors testifying in favor of property rights; one ignoramus said the city "might as well get rid of everything and start over." Gentrification came up, with the owner's realtor referring to the area's "safety issues," a subtly racist dog whistle, prompting another neighbor, Joshua Duran, to cry foul: "I am concerned that our history is being scraped by people who have no investment in our community." The DLPC voted unanimously for preservation, but city council voted seven to four against it. Espinoza commented, "This was one little fragment [of Jefferson Park's historical fabric] that could have remained, and I'm sorry to let my community down." The Hoyt House was scraped in favor of "slot homes," an architectural form later banned by city council.[10]

THE HUT

Built in 1901 at 1980 Albion Street, the ironically named "Hut," with seven bedrooms and large entertainment spaces, sprawled over five thousand square feet. Its builder, Charles Alfred Johnson, was a Boston transplant who had risen to business and social prominence. He befriended prickly Baron

Allois Gillaume Eugene von Winkler, who harbored dreams of creating Denver's finest suburb, Park Hill Ranch, on land he owned east of City Park. In 1898, the Baron committed suicide, and Johnson, one of his few friends, was named executor. He sold von Winkler's properties to a syndicate headed by David B. Gamble, heir to the Procter & Gamble fortune, and Gamble soon fulfilled von Winkler's vision, marketing lots to Denver's upper middle class. Liking the area, Johnson bought an entire block and hired Theodore Boal to design a home for himself and his new bride, Anne.

Although Boal was known for opulent neoclassical designs, including the contemporaneous Grant-Humphreys Mansion and slightly later Crawford Hill Mansion (both extant), Johnson wanted something different. In 1901, Gustav Stickley launched *The Craftsman* magazine, popularizing the American Craftsman style, a "total design" aesthetic in which every element—architecture, interior design and landscape—worked together, creating a distinctly modern style, emphasizing simplicity and domesticity, markedly different from both Victorian clutter and neoclassical purity. Boal's design exemplified the Craftsman movement, with its broad, deep enclosed veranda, low-slung roofline and interior built-in elements emphasizing the natural and handmade. It also incorporated elements of the New England Vernacular style, popular at the time and reminding Johnson of home.

Johnson lived in the Hut for a quarter century, hosting frequent parties. He was president of the Denver Chamber of Commerce, held membership in several other booster organizations and worked with Warwick Downing

South façade of the Hut, circa 1905, with Ash Street running northward behind it. *Susan Keats collection.*

in establishing the Denver Mountain Parks System. Some Massachusetts relations came to live, buying adjacent lots from him and building houses. Anne died in 1914, and while Johnson was volunteering in France during World War I, he met Alice Gifford Phillips and married her in 1920. After buying a ranch near Sedalia, in 1925–26 they built a summer home, hiring Merrill and Burnham Hoyt to design a twenty-four-room Scottish castle they named Charlford after their son Charles and Alice's son by a previous marriage, Gifford. Johnson died in 1954, and this Douglas County property, along with an adjacent one, became Cherokee Ranch, where Mildred "Tweet" Kimball bred Santa Gertrudis cattle.

The Hut met its end in 2019. A longtime owner had not maintained it, and significant sums of money would have been required to bring it up to contemporary standards. A realtor purchased it in 2018, applying for a certificate of non-historic status. Concerned neighbors filed with the DLPC for landmark status and Historic Denver, Inc. looked for solutions. While the realtor said he was open to selling the property to another buyer, all efforts failed and the house was demolished. As of this book's writing, the lot remains for sale. The Hut lives on, however, as a tile mural in one of the bathrooms of Cherokee Castle, open to the public.[11]

KITTREDGE CASTLE

Like Central Park, the set of twenty-first-century neighborhoods developed on treeless former Stapleton Airport land, Baron Walter B. von Richthofen built his town of Montclair on bald prairie. Richthofen dreamed of a morally upright, upper- and upper-middle-class community enjoying clean air and mountain views, a "health suburb" five miles east of and five hundred feet higher than 1880s Denver. Unlike Central Park, linked to everywhere by freeway and rail, the difficulty of getting to Montclair greatly inhibited development. Builder and financier Charles Marble Kittredge, who believed in Richthofen's dream for an American Carlsbad, demonstrated his support by building a counterpart to the baron's own German-style castle (extant today), a three-story English-style one, complete with crenelated parapet. In the early 1890s, before the Panic of 1893, Kittredge utilized his home in marketing lots. "Not the Montclair Art Gallery," one advertisement headlined, "for which it has been taken by many, but simply a dwelling which you may at any time inspect free of charge by taking the new Montclair Electric," a streetcar line that failed

The Kittredge Castle, circa 1890. *Denver Public Library, Western History Collection, X-26702.*

to completely erase the distance from Denver. Kittredge Park, between 8th and 9th Avenues and Oneida and Olive Streets, honors the castle's memory; it stood at the park's southern end facing 8th.

Kittredge is remembered today for his namesake downtown building on 16th Street and Glenarm Place and for the Bear Creek Canyon resort town, Kittredge, he founded. Yet earlier generations knew him as well for this eccentric structure designed by John James Huddart and built of Castle Rock rhyolite. Broader than it was deep, it had twelve major rooms, including a top-floor dining room with a wall of windows looking south to Pikes Peak. Putting this room on the top floor was eccentric; purportedly, Kittredge disliked kitchen noise and odors, but the kitchen was also on this floor. This configuration made the house perfect for entertaining, its ground floor devoted to large public rooms, including a library, art gallery and conservatory. The house cost $80,000 to build, and Kittredge spent the same on furnishings and landscaped the grounds with evergreens and lilacs. The 1893 Panic devastated Kittredge; he lost control of his downtown building, and that year, he sold the castle and its fifteen lots to John H. Nichols for just $40,000. A 1906 *Denver Post* article eulogized the era: "That castle at

Montclair, builded by Charles Kittredge in 1890, was a kind of metaphor somehow, a thing of stone and oak and bastions....It expressed correctly what men thought before the panic of '93 blew into thin air many another man's 'castle in Spain' higher even than that of Montclair." Kittredge later returned to Montclair, building "tuberculosis houses" with carpenter Dennis Tirsway, but never again lived in his castle. He died in 1940.

Was there something odd about the house that caused people to live in it only briefly? "The lonely footsteps of a caretaker have echoed gloomily in its vacant halls of recent years," the same *Post* journalist wrote. Nichols later sold the house to a "Mrs. Eddy Smith," likely Amelia Eddy-Smith, widow of smelter magnate Edward Eddy, but she never lived in it, as she had returned to England after Eddy's death. In 1906, Colonel William Edgar Hughes, selling the Fletcher Mansion, paid just $20,000 for Kittredge Castle. He and son-in-law John Springer, who owned nearby 770 Olive Street, planned to expand the outbuilding, built in the same style, into a large stable for Hughes's fine horses, but first they had to evict the castle's tenant, an eccentric Scotchman named George O.L. Davidson. Backed by a $50,000 investment from a Lord Armstrong, Davidson and his wife had rented the castle in 1905. Behind it, Davidson erected a fifteen-foot-high fence and began constructing a huge "airship"; by the time Hughes bought the property the airship stood seventy-five feet high and was the "talk of Montclair." He apparently worked out a deal with Springer, renting 770 Olive and removing his unfinished airship to that house's grounds. Nothing came of Davidson's fantastical invention; his wife divorced him in 1907 after Lord Armstrong shut off the money, and no Denver citizens stepped up to provide funding. In 1908, with the airship almost ready for its test flight, its engine exploded, and that was that.

Hughes did not long remain in Kittredge Castle, which he renamed Sunland Castle. In late 1907, he announced he would return to his Texas ranch permanently, using Sunland as a summer home only. He was just then gaining custody from Springer of his beloved granddaughter Annie Clifton Springer. Her mother, Eliza, Hughes's only daughter, had died in 1904 shortly after Springer lost the mayoral election to Robert W. Speer, and in April 1907, Springer had remarried, to the twenty-years-younger (and ultimately unfaithful) Isabel Patterson Folck. This second marriage caused a rift between Hughes and Springer. Instead of Texas, Hughes relocated to tony Forest Park in St. Louis. In 1912, after Springer divorced Isabel following the infamous 1911 murder of her lover Tony Von Phul by her other lover Frank Henwood in The Brown Palace's Marble Bar, the men

The Kittredge Castle (Holland Hall) entry, 1948. *Denver Public Library, Western History Collection, X-26699; photograph by Orin A. Sealy.*

reconciled. Hughes never deserted Colorado, retaining Kittredge Castle and a large Perry Park ranch, but instead of returning to Montclair, he bought land near the Denver Country Club and built two houses: 320 High Street for himself and his wife and 300 High next door for Annie and her new husband, Lafayette Hughes (no relation).

Hughes could not return anyway: he had turned over the castle to Dean Arthur C. Peck of the City Temple Institutional Society, who in 1909 moved the Peck Training School for Girls into it, renaming it Clifton Hughes Training School for Girls, for Hughes's wife, Annie Clifton Hughes. Nearby residents protested the change in use, and Hughes and Peck nearly succumbed to their complaints but ultimately moved the school, founded in 1892 and located near the State Capitol, to the morally and physically healthier climate of Montclair. Neighbors feared for property values: the girls, ages nine through fourteen, were often charity cases, although fifteen dollars per month was charged to parents who could afford it. This was not a school for "incorrigibles." "The only crime of which these girls can be charged," Hughes proclaimed, "is that of not having been born with gold spoons in their mouths." Peck remodeled the outbuilding into a gymnasium, and second-floor bedrooms became dormitories, with the lunchroom upstairs. Girls were soon learning their ABCs along with music, drawing and home economics. (The society also operated a boys' boarding school in the Belle Lennox Hall near the former Oakes Home.)

One month prior to his 1918 death, Hughes deeded the property to the school. A front-page *Denver Post* obituary by Gene Fowler estimated him Denver's second-wealthiest man after Lawrence Phipps. He also endowed the school with $52,000. It operated for several years, eventually renamed Holland Hall, for Mary E. Holland, a children's rights activist and executive secretary of the Colorado Children's Aid Society, which converted the school into a home for teenage girls. Holland was a crusader, in 1927 calling for a "Bill of Rights for childhood" to secure better lives for all juveniles. In 1935, about twenty girls lived here when a fire broke out in the basement; the damage was repaired. Kittredge Castle enjoyed one final moment of glory when, in 1953, James Stewart and June Allyson arrived in Denver to film the Universal-International picture *The Glenn Miller Story*. Director Anthony Mann shot scenes at Holland Hall, as well as in a Lowry Air Force Base hangar and Elitch Gardens' Trocadero Ballroom. Two years later, the Archdiocese of Denver purchased Holland Hall, along with the rest of the block, and demolished everything. The archdiocese never used the land, and by the 1970s, Montclair residents were tired of a weed-filled lot, petitioning the city to buy the property to create Kittredge Park.[12]

McFarland–Vick Roy–McGill Mansion

The story of the fourteen-room mansion at 1474 Gilpin Street at Colfax Avenue—designed by Robert G. Balcomb or his partner, Eugene Remich Rice—has been largely forgotten, although many Balcomb and Rice works remain in the nearby Wyman Historic District. Its gray rusticated rhyolite stone façade, trimmed in red sandstone, with powerful Richardsonian Romanesque arches, stained glass, four chimneys and whimsical Queen Anne elements, including towers, dormers and balconies, mark it as one of the firm's most elaborate works. The mansion's life was brief: the city issued the building permit in 1890 and the demolition permit just four decades later. Its construction cost was $25,000 at a time when average houses could be built for $2,000 to $5,000. G.R. Griffett built it, and when it was complete, Austin McFarland took ownership and moved in with his wife and twin daughters. Note that others have called this the Gustofsen-McGill Mansion. Although the name Gustofsen (in several variant spellings) was not unknown in Denver during the house's four decades, this writer finds no evidence that anyone named Gustofsen ever lived in it or owned it.

"Everybody in the West has heard the familiar name of Austin McFarland, general ticket agent…of the Denver and Rio Grande [Railroad]…the biggest star in the galaxy of Western ticket agents," proclaimed the *Rocky Mountain News* in 1889. With prominent forehead, broad waxed moustache and goatee, and favoring the sort of narrow bow tie with long tails associated with Kentucky gentlemen like himself, "Colonel Mac" McFarland supervised the railroad's busy city ticket office at 17th and Larimer Streets, the summit of a transportation career that began after fighting for the Confederacy during the Civil War. An avid art collector, McFarland frequently displayed his latest purchases in the D&RG ticket office for public enjoyment; he also invested in real estate, building, in partnership with other railroad executives, several mansions on Pennsylvania Street. McFarland and his family occupied their new home in February 1892, and by March, the house was already hosting dinner parties, including one honoring Colonel William F. "Buffalo Bill" Cody.

McFarland lost the house less than two years later. The Panic of 1893 decimated fortunes, but it was his firing from the railroad that spring that forced him to sell. He had long operated a side business brokering railroad tickets. McFarland would vend a round-trip ticket to a one-way traveler; the passenger would then cheaply sell the return ticket to another broker in Chicago, who would resell it at face value, dividing the profits with

The McFarland–Vick Roy–McGill Mansion, circa 1893. *Denver Public Library, Western History Collection, WHJ-811; photograph by William Henry Jackson.*

McFarland. This put him into direct competition with independent ticket brokers, and after years of losing business to an insider, they threatened action against the line. McFarland practiced this openly and claimed no dishonesty. A year after his firing, the railroad rehired him, but he had sold his home the previous November.

The buyer was Miranda Eliza Vick Roy. She was married to Roy Thomas Vick Roy (a compound surname), sire of a large family that included baker Lucien Bonaparte Vick Roy, Denver city clerk and GOP operative Joseph Jerome Vick Roy and Union Pacific Railroad chief dispatcher (for Denver) and El Jebel Mystic Shrine Grand Potentate Alonzo Ferdinand Vick Roy. No Vick Roy family member occupied the house, but two years after buying it, Miranda transferred ownership to Joseph, who continued living with her at 2211 Curtis Street. Possibly the Vick Roys bought the house as an investment, leasing to well-heeled tenants, but it may also have been vacant for a time; a 1906 article referred to it as "the 'haunted' house of Capitol Hill."

Haunted or not, the house's next owner was inarguably its most colorful—yet some of that "color" may have been ugly. James Christian McGill's Denver period is well chronicled in newspapers, particularly in the sports pages where doting columnists Otto Floto (*Post*) and Pyke Johnson (*News*) christened the young, blond, blue-eyed, clean-shaven, small-statured man "Jimmy." His uncle George E. Smith, "Pittsburg Phil," one of the best-known horse race "plungers" of his era, had amassed a fortune by trading in, and betting on, Thoroughbreds; so famous was he in that world that the 1916 Kentucky Derby winner was named for him, and his posthumously published *Maxims* inspires professional handicappers today. Smith, who had raised McGill after his parents passed, developed tuberculosis and died in early 1905. His $3,250,000 estate was divided evenly between five relatives, including his favorite, James McGill. Suddenly flush at twenty-five, McGill relocated to Denver. He knew Colorado somewhat, having often frequented "Little London," Colorado Springs; why he chose Denver is unknown. An early report claimed he came for his health, as he was rumored to have caught tuberculosis from his uncle, but he assured Floto that he was feeling fine. He rented a Park Hill home at 2275 Paloma (now Ash) Street.

In November 1905 came news that he had not arrived alone but with a bride, the former Pauline Rowland of Cincinnati. They had met in Asheville, North Carolina, where his uncle had stayed in a sanitarium, and had married secretly in 1904. There were multiple reasons for discretion, including his uncle's maxim: "A man who wishes to be successful [in betting] cannot divide his attentions between horses and women." Smith had secured a promise from McGill to not marry "on pain of disinheritance"; when he married, his uncle still lived. Yet there was another reason for secrecy: McGill had previously pledged his heart to another woman. In 1902, he had traveled with Smith to San Francisco, where he met Estelle F. Del Poso, "a beautiful young Spanish maiden" in one account or "a woman of the half-world" (prostitute) in another. Young men make impulsive choices, and McGill, having fallen in love, invited her to follow him back to New York City. There they cohabitated until November 1904, when he accompanied his uncle to Asheville. He promised her that once his uncle died they would marry, but after he met Pauline, he deserted Estelle. Coming to Denver took him out of Estelle's orbit, but she soon discovered his whereabouts. In August 1906, she filed a breach-of-promise suit, seeking $50,000. She faced an uphill battle, made harder by Denver judge George Allen's apparent prejudice against her, likely fueled by McGill's well-paid lawyers, who secured affidavits testifying to her "immoral character" and her "reaping enormous profits" from her presumed trade. McGill, perennially lucky, was off the hook when Estelle suddenly died of tuberculosis in April 1907.

By this time, James and Pauline McGill were ensconced at 1474 Gilpin, having purchased it from the Vick Roys in December 1905 for $20,000. An avid "automobilist," "known as the owner of probably more automobiles than any man in the state," McGill hired Harold and Viggo Baerressen to design a four-car garage and remodel the house, with a budget of $10,000. The couple occupied the mansion in April 1906. Pauline made friends with a wide circle, society columnists chronicling parties she attended and gave, her theater attendance and other doings. The *News* described her as a "petite beauty with exquisite coloring, fine eyes, masses of light brown hair and a bewitching smile…modestly attired and entirely unconscious of the admiration she elicited." Sometimes James accompanied her, but frequently her name appeared alone. While comfortable socializing, his main interest was sports, not just horse racing, and his name often appeared on the automobile pages. He bought and sold frequently, always seeking the latest and fastest models. In 1908, he paid $6,000 for a luxurious ("a veritable palace on wheels") six-cylinder Thomas Flyer capable of sixty miles per hour. A similar model won the 1908 New York to Paris Auto Race, and McGill could be seen flying down primitive Colorado roads in his. He could afford a chauffeur but preferred the thrill of driving himself. In 1909, he formed a partnership with John E. Fry, opening Fry & McGill Motor Supply Company on the ground floor of the Majestic Building. Aiming to equip Denver motorists with a complete selection, it even sold driving clothing and later added motorcycles.

McGill is best remembered for his next act: in December 1909, he paid $10,000 for a half-interest in the Denver Bears baseball team, then playing in the Western League. This team had suffered from its previous owner's unwillingness to invest in talent; in 1909, it had finished near the bottom of the eight-team league with 69 wins and 82 losses, just above the Lincoln Greenbackers and Pueblo Indians. McGill's willingness to pay high salaries to top players manifested itself immediately: in 1910, the Bears (nicknamed the Grizzlies by sportswriters) finished in second place, and the 1911 season, with McGill now owning 100 percent of the franchise, saw them top the league with 111 wins and only 54 losses. This winning season was legendary; in 2001, two experts ranked the 1911 Grizzlies at number twenty-two in a list of "100 Best Minor League Teams" of the prior century. At season end, visiting President William Howard Taft presented McGill with a loving cup subscribed by grateful Denver baseball fans. McGill, aided by manager Jack Hendricks, then achieved a "three-peat," winning the pennant again in 1912 and 1913. The Grizzlies played at Broadway Park, a triangular plot between Broadway, Bannock Street, 6th Avenue and (today's) Speer Boulevard, with home plate near 6th and Bannock. McGill expanded grandstands and provided more parking, even though most spectators arrived by streetcar. McGill generously allowed amateur teams to play and distributed free tickets to *Denver Post* newsboys.

McGill's interest in Denver began waning in 1913, after he bought another team, the Indianapolis Indians of the American Association. He paid a minor-league record price, $175,000, for it and shifted his focus to Indianapolis, transferring Hendricks there as manager and bringing on John F. "Jack" Coffey as Denver manager. The Bears finished in second place in 1914 and 1915, but toward the end of the 1915 season, Coffey acrimoniously quit over a "personal matter." Sportswriters were mystified about why two apparently friendly associates fell out but got their answer when Coffey and his wife, Lorean, filed suit against McGill, seeking $20,000 each. She claimed that on August 25, 1915, McGill had spotted her walking toward the ballpark and offered to take her for a drive. He said they would swing by his house for his wife, but Lorean grew concerned when he seemed to drive aimlessly, not toward his Capitol Hill home. She said he drove "straight into the country…out beyond the Agnes Memorial Sanitarium," where he "made advances," which she rebuffed. Then, she said, he pulled her from the car. She managed to break free, but "he chased her over the prairie until he caught her." Newspapers would not describe what happened next, but after he drove off, she walked back several miles "in a disheveled state," her clothing torn and her body bruised, to the nearest streetcar line. When asked whether the charges were true, McGill scoffed, calling them "ridiculous." He claimed overpowering her was impossible: "Do I look like I was even physically able to do what she charges? Mrs. Coffey is a pretty big woman—and I believe that if anything of that kind ever happened and there was a fight, it wouldn't be Mrs. Coffey who's been disheveled—but the other fellow." *The Post*'s accompanying photograph revealed her to be a slender woman, neither large nor tall.

Exactly what happened is unknown. McGill's attorneys claimed they could find no witness to substantiate her claim of being in a disheveled state and riding a streetcar. Three months after filing suit, Jack and Lorean settled out of court for $1,000 and his release from contract. He lacked McGill's fortune; what seems likeliest is that without income, and under contract to the Bears, he could not get another baseball job, and he needed to settle or go bankrupt. He and Lorean relocated to California, where he worked with a new team. Alternatively, McGill could have been speaking truth, that he was victim of a grift. However, he now no longer owned the team, having sold it to Hugh L. Jones. Perhaps the sale had nothing to do with the Coffey suit—he had been seeking a buyer since 1914—but the timing, and that it was sold to a twenty-year friend, is curious. Visiting Denver a few months after the settlement, he took in a Bears game, telling a reporter that he "consider[ed] Denver as his home town," but within the year, he had sold 1473 Gilpin to unknown "out-of-town persons," and on a 1917 visit, he told *The Post* that his permanent summer home was Indianapolis, with winters in Southern California. What of Pauline McGill, the wife who had endured long absences as her husband traveled on baseball business and endured the humiliation of the Coffey episode? She and James had had three children during their marriage, daughters Fay and Pauline and son Russell. They remained married, and the couple relocated to San Diego, where she died in 1931. James McGill died in Pasadena in 1972, aged ninety-one.

In 1933, the magnificent house was destroyed and replaced with a gasoline station operated by Raymond T. Young. This was later demolished for a car dealership, which eventually became a grocery and is currently a dollar store.[13]

RAINE HOUSE

The humblest house in this book, a two-story, Dutch gambrel-roofed cottage facing sideways on its lot at 4433 West 29th Avenue, attracted few protests when it came down in 2015, together with neighboring houses, so a developer could inflict an unsightly two-story commercial building on the neighborhood. When in 2008 its owner applied for a certificate of non-historic status, the DLPC staff found no historic worth. When that five-year permit expired, no one reexamined the earlier conclusion. Yet this little abode was once home to one of America's most popular novelists of the first half of the twentieth century, William MacLeod Raine. It was here that he began writing western-themed short stories and novels, the first of which, *Wyoming*, was published in 1908. Ultimately, he wrote more than eighty novels, with twenty adapted into Hollywood movies and many translated into foreign languages. During World War I, 500,000 copies of his novels entertained soldiers in France. Over his lifetime, over 19 million copies of his books were sold to avid readers. Denverites were proud to boast a famous author in their midst, yet fame is fleeting.

Born in London in 1871 to Scottish parents ("if you stick a hatpin in me deep enough I bleed oatmeal and haggis," he joked), he immigrated to the United States in 1881 when his father took up ranching in Arkansas, later moving to Texas. In that state, Raine learned to love outdoor life, absorbing

The William MacLeod Raine House. *Drawing by Shari Myers.*

the cowboy culture that would animate his later career. Graduating from Oberlin College in 1894, he moved to Seattle, where he taught school. Seattle's damp climate disagreed with him: Raine developed tuberculosis and came to Denver for the cure. Seeking more exciting work, he joined the *Denver Republican* as a reporter; he later moved to *The Denver Post*, where he wrote Sunday supplement features, and finally to the *Rocky Mountain News*. Politically progressive, he wrote editorials supporting municipal ownership of the Denver Union Water Company and for charter amendments that gave Colorado the initiative and referendum; he referred to these latter causes as "democracy in the saddle," proclaiming they would give citizens a true democratic voice. With his connections at the *American Magazine* (including Lincoln Steffens), he helped publicize nationally his friend Judge Benjamin Barr Lindsey's pioneering juvenile justice reforms. In 1911, the University of Colorado regents appointed Raine to a journalism teaching post, and in 1914, he was one of four top winners of a *Post* essay contest on the topic "Buffalo Bill: What Has He Done for America?" with Cody himself awarding the prizes. In 1916, with Denver voters considering reinstating the strong-mayor form of government and reelecting Robert W. Speer as mayor, Raine again editorialized, urging voters to not be "quitters" in the project of democracy by allowing the corporations' tool (Speer) to take power again.

In 1922, Raine published *Tangled Trails*, a detective story set in Denver; prior to book publication, the *News* serialized it, advertising, "Follow the lady of the violet perfume along Curtis street; accompany the hero as he trails the villain along Welton street; go with the distracted heroine on a hurried auto trip across the Fourteenth street viaduct, along Federal boulevard; witness the unraveling of the mystery in the office of the slain man in the Equitable building." Denver loved it, and him, and he loved Denver back: "Why do I live in Denver? Because the mile high town is my town. Because it is the best town on earth. Because it is the heart of the West."

Raine married Pearl Langley in 1905, and as newlyweds, they moved into 4433 West 29th; its building permit had been taken out by Pearl, who taught at Edison School at West 30th Avenue and Quitman Street. They lived there through at least the mid-1910s, the house's first full decade; by 1920, they lived elsewhere. Pearl died in 1922, and Raine, after remarrying, relocated at least twice before settling into the Country Club neighborhood at 150 Race Street in about 1928, where he died in 1954. Late in life, he was one of eleven founding members of the Denver Posse of Westerners, a history study group still alive today.[14]

Chapter 2

COMMERCIAL LANDMARKS

Ernest and Cranmer Building

Standing eight stories tall on the southern corner of 17th and Curtis Streets, the office block built by and named for Finis Plumley Ernest and William Henry Harrison Cranmer exemplified the transition of Denver from small regional town to important American city. Its design, by Frank E. Edbrooke, took cues from contemporaneous work in Chicago, its tripartite composition of base, shaft and capital resembling a classical column and its structure based on iron columns rather than loadbearing exterior walls. Edbrooke, who had come from Chicago in 1879 to supervise construction of the Tabor Block (designed by his brother Willoughby), was at the peak of his career, creating one fine commercial building after another, including some of his best-known extant downtown buildings, the Oxford Hotel, Masonic Building and his masterpiece, The Brown Palace Hotel.

In pre-air-conditioned times, large buildings had light wells, allowing better ventilation. Typically alley-fronting, they were built of less expensive brick than that used on street-facing walls, but to convey this building's first-class status, Edbrooke centered the light well on the 17th Street façade, utilizing more expensive brick, fancy stone column capitals and other pricy details. This also broke up the mass, making it seem less bulky. Each half was divided into three bays, with five-story pilasters between them culminating in dramatic arched windows on the seventh floor. The Curtis façade was similar, without the light well. The first two floors were finished in locally quarried

The Ernest and Cranmer Building, circa 1890. *History Colorado, 20100049; photograph by William Henry Jackson.*

Caricature by F. Finch ("Doc Bird") of architect Frank E. Edbrooke, 1909. *Author's collection.*

red sandstone, with upper floors in red-brown brick. Local brick would not suffice—these were manufactured in St. Louis. There were two entrances; the entry on 17th was through a deep Richardsonian arch topped by a carved triangular pediment. The Ernest and Cranmer Building stood proudly among its 17th Street peers, which included the Quincy and Cooper Buildings (also by Edbrooke) on other corners of the Curtis intersection and the nearby Boston and Equitable Buildings, designed by arguably more prestigious out-of-town architects.

As architecturally interesting as the E&C (as it was abbreviated) was, the lives of its builders were even more fascinating. "Fine" Ernest—only strangers addressed him as Finis—was born on an Arkansas slave plantation to "sternly religious parents" in 1843. His father raised beef cattle, giving Fine an early education in them. During the Civil War, he joined the Rebel army as a private under General Sterling Price, seeing action in the Trans-Mississippi Theater. Either curiosity or love of adventure found him in Mexico in 1865, serving in General Porfirio Díaz's army, fighting Habsburg emperor Maximilian I. He remained in Mexico through Benito Juárez's election and Maximilian's execution, which he personally witnessed. Crossing the Rio Grande, he made his way to Palo Pinto County, Texas, west of Fort Worth, beginning a lucrative career raising cattle. Also living in Palo Pinto was his future business partner, William H.H. Cranmer; they may have formed their friendship then. In 1868, Ernest first encountered Colorado, driving a herd over the Pecos Trail. With rustling increasingly problematic in Palo Pinto, he began shifting his operation to New Mexico, where he married cattleman's daughter Elizabeth Stockton; they had four children before her early death in 1876. In 1874, he began running three thousand head on part of the famous Maxwell Land Grant in Colfax County but ran afoul of a local mob and decided to look farther north. One of his Palo Pinto friends, John Nathan Hittson, had previously established Six Springs Ranch on Bijou Creek near Deer Trail southeast of Denver and began acquiring water rights. By now, Ernest's herd numbered seven thousand, and he bought a ranch not far from Hittson's, joining other former Texas cattlemen, including Cranmer. In 1880, Ernest remarried, to Salina Virginia Hittson, John's daughter. She gave birth to five children and treated his original four as her own. The Ernests, like their Deer Trail friends, spent winters in Denver, buying a house at 1579 Emerson Street and entering society. Ernest's herd kept growing; by 1885, he owned thirty-six thousand head.

Fine Ernest was also a gambler's gambler, despite his strait-laced upbringing. His nephew George Cranmer described Fine as "well over six feet tall and of a very powerful build with great, powerful hands. He had a sharp sense of humor and loved to tell stories, but he could assume an inscrutable 'poker face.'" Once, he played a poker game with three Cubans visiting Denver. After playing all night, he returned home, and while his wife complained about his gambling them into the poorhouse, he pulled $77,000 in cash winnings from various pockets. Another tale involved railroad magnate Edward Henry Harriman. Stopping in Denver after traveling to San Francisco, he heard of Ernest's prowess with cards and invited him to accompany him back to California. Harriman had lost a fortune to cardsharps and wanted revenge; Ernest provided it. Even at Ernest's death, his friends remembered him as a gambler as much as a cattleman or real estate man.

William H.H. Cranmer was a year older, born in 1842 in Cooper County, Missouri. Like Ernest, he joined the Confederate army at war's outbreak. He was decorated for action in Missouri and Kansas and rose to captain. Postwar, he moved to Palo Pinto County, where he worked as Hittson's ranch foreman. When Hittson relocated to Deer Trail, Cranmer established his own Three Ring Ranch at Elbert. In 1874, he married Hittson's daughter Martha Jane, who would bear seven children. Joining Denver society in winter, they commissioned Frank Edbrooke to design a home at 928 East 17th Avenue. Cranmer, Hittson and Ernest together controlled water rights across a wide swath of eastern Colorado, from Fort Morgan to the Arkansas River and from Denver to Kansas.

In 1886, Ernest and Cranmer liquidated most of their herds, freeing up cash. They had decided to make a permanent mark on their adopted city, paying $12,000 for five lots at 17th and Curtis, formerly a residential zone. This corner had been home to Judge Amos Steck since 1860. Steck had served as Denver's second mayor and as school board president and had filled other civic and commercial roles. Construction began in May 1889 and was largely complete by the end of 1890. In August 1890, they placed advertisements seeking bids from booksellers to equip a large law library on the eighth floor. Demand for prestige space was high, and the building was filled almost immediately, its tenants attracted not only to its modernity and beauty but also to fireproof vaults on each floor. The prime ground-floor corner space housed Denver National Bank (Finis P. Ernest, president) and, on the Curtis side, the E. & C. Restaurant & Bar. Attorneys constituted the largest share of the tenants, but also present were insurance companies, stockbrokers, railroad companies, investment firms, advertising agencies and other businesses.

Sadly not present was Cranmer, who passed away on December 2, 1890. His estate continued to own a half share in the building for years, providing his widow a healthy income. Their children grew up and married into Denver's elite families, including those of McPhee, Russell and Coors. Their fourth child, George Ernest Cranmer, proved consequential. Dubbed "Denver's First Citizen" by poet/historian Thomas Hornsby Ferril, he entered civic life in 1935 after years as a stockbroker. He successfully managed Benjamin F. Stapleton's mayoral campaign, running for a third term after being defeated four years earlier for reelection after his second. In return, Stapleton named Cranmer manager of parks and improvements, and in that capacity, he bought Red Rocks Park, built its world-famous amphitheater and developed Denver's Winter Park ski area. His wife, Jean Chappell Cranmer, similarly contributed, co-founding the Denver Civic Symphony (ancestor of today's Colorado Symphony) and, with her brother Delos Chappell Jr., donating their parents' mansion, Chappell House, to the Denver Art Museum, providing its first permanent home. George and Jean Cranmer's home still stands, a Jules Jacques Benoit Benedict design on the eastern side of Cranmer Park in Hilltop.

Ernest lived twenty-two years after his partner's death. Although he continued investing in Denver real estate, he ventured elsewhere. He bought 750 acres across the Mississippi from downtown St. Louis, developing much of East St. Louis, Illinois, including a commercial district named Denverside. His Alta Sita neighborhood there originally had streets named for his Denver friends. With Henry M. Porter and other Coloradans, he developed a Galveston, Texas subdivision, although that proved less lucrative. In 1901, his wife was named one of the "lady managers" of the 1904 Louisiana Purchase Exhibition, the St. Louis World's Fair, and in 1903, the Ernests moved to East St. Louis permanently, with frequent trips to Colorado for business and pleasure (favoring Manitou Springs vacations). In 1908, Ernest sold his share of the building to Jerome S. Riche and realtors Bennett and Myers. In 1909, he unsuccessfully attempted to buy, with partner Maxcy

Tabor, The Brown Palace, which Tabor managed (Ernest had once been a favorite poker partner of Maxcy's father, Horace). In 1910, an automobile struck Ernest as he crossed 17th Street. He survived and recuperated, but his health declined. In 1912, traveling on a train from Colorado to Illinois, he suffered a stroke and died after reaching home. His body came back to Denver for the funeral and interment at Fairmount Cemetery. He left an estate valued at $5 million, distributing most of it prior to his death.

In 1959, Colorado National Bank, located across the alley on the 17th and Champa corner, bought the Ernest and Cranmer, the first step in assembling the entire block; it would later buy the empty May Company department store and S.H. Kress store. The bank was engaging in private urban renewal, years before DURA established its Skyline Project. CNB demolished the Ernest and Cranmer and the other structures in 1963–65. Its plan was to erect skyscrapers, although it initially plopped a drive-through bank onto the former Ernest and Cranmer site. Eventually, CNB commissioned Japanese American architect Minoru Yamasaki to design a twenty-six-story high-rise tower in place of the E&C, completed in 1975. A decent building of its time, it cannot match the elegance of its predecessor.[15]

Interstate Trust Company Building

In 1969, Vincent Scully, in *American Architecture and Urbanism*, characterized urban renewal, then at the peak of its destructive power in American downtowns, as being "wielded mostly by certain kinds of lawyers and civil administrators, full of lies and dodges, with hearts like small stones." Two years later, attorney George Louis Creamer declared, "Urban renewal is a very evil thing. It is the most destructive force which ever hit American cities and Denver." Creamer knew from experience; he was then working for several Auraria businessmen fighting DURA's plans to build a higher-education complex where their buildings stood, but previously, he had fought DURA at one of Denver's prime downtown intersections, 16th and Lawrence Streets. If ever there was an example of misguided, retrograde intentions overcoming thoughtful, progressive ones, it was the fate of the Interstate Trust Company Building, victim of DURA's "clean slate" mentality in its Skyline Project. Unlike most other landmarks demolished for Skyline, this building's owners were committed to its preservation, renovation and reuse but could not overcome the collective will of Denver's power brokers.

The People's Bank Building, circa 1890. *History Colorado, 20102520; photograph by William Henry Jackson.*

Designed by Frank E. Edbrooke and towering nine stories high, it featured a two-story rusticated red sandstone base with a two-story arched entry on 16th. Above these rose seven stories of red pressed brick, with arched windows on the fourth and eighth floors; elaborately carved capitals divided those on the eighth. A more sober top floor and elaborate brick cornice above it capped off the design; a "stylistically retardataire corner tower" (really more of an elaborate finial), in the words of architectural historian Richard Brettell, punctured the skyline above the intersection. Brettell declared it "was among Edbrooke's most successful buildings of any size in any material." He was correct; its loss made Denver less interesting.

The People's National Savings Bank built it, and in its earliest years, it was known by that name. Mortimer J. Lawrence founded this institution in 1888, during the long boom that preceded the Panic of 1893; among its stockholders was retailer John Jay Joslin. Initially, People's occupied the Londoner Block at 1640 Arapahoe Street (another Skyline victim) before moving to its newly completed facility in 1890, by which time a sister institution had been organized as People's National Bank. Retail shops occupied the ground floor with the banking hall on the second. One of the earliest bank runs during the Panic occurred here on May 4, 1893, but Denver leaders convinced its depositors that People's was sound, temporarily staving off doom. It was over on July 17, when People's declared insolvency; the savings bank went into receivership, while the national bank, after recapitalization, lingered on five more years until it too failed.

Banking returned to the building in 1902, when Colonel William Edgar Hughes, his son-in-law John W. Springer and several investors, including retailers David May and Leopold Henry Guldman (whose department stores stood at the same intersection), formed the Continental Trust Company. Hughes and Springer, as described in chapter 1, were wealthy cattlemen originally based in Texas; Hughes's operation was the Continental Cattle Company, likely why he gave the bank the name "Continental." They had bought the building for $250,000 in 1901 from George C. Schleier with the specific plan of chartering a bank. Hughes was no greenhorn to the industry; he had previously directed banks in St. Louis and Dallas. The Continental Trust Company Building, as it was now called, was still considered one of Denver's finest office buildings, fully leased and home to myriad businesses. Hughes remained president for several years, but after he and Springer fell out following Springer's remarriage to Isabel Patterson Folck, Hughes sold his shares and Springer became president of Continental Trust. After Springer divorced Isabel, he and Hughes reconciled, Hughes returning to Denver and reassuming the presidency.

Meanwhile, Interstate Savings Bank conducted bustling business from humble quarters at 15th and Stout. Like People's Bank, this institution began by accepting small deposits from ordinary people, and like People's, its directors decided they could make greater profits by taking out a second charter, not as a national bank but as a trust company, which they did in 1913. The new charter was likely the work of Frank Newton Briggs, who owned a large share and served as Interstate's president. Born in Windsor, Colorado, in 1870 to George A. Briggs, an 1859 pioneer cattleman, Frank Briggs came to Denver in 1879 and as a teenager worked for his uncle William Newton Byers, who had founded the *Rocky Mountain News* in 1859 and was then serving as Denver's postmaster (Briggs's mother was Rachel Byers, William's sister). As a young man, Briggs struck out for Grand County, where he farmed and became postmaster at Hot Sulphur Springs. During the 1890s Cripple Creek gold rush, he relocated to Victor, where he bought its newspaper, the *Victor Record*. He sold it in 1901, returned to Grand County and opened banks at Hot Sulphur Springs and Fraser. In 1908, he relocated to Denver, buying a share of Interstate Savings Bank and becoming its cashier. Also during this time, with some partners he bought land northeast of Greeley and founded the town of Briggsdale. In 1911, Interstate's directors named him president, as he had been "largely responsible for its growth" over the previous three years.

Doc Bird caricature of Interstate Trust Company president Franklin Newton Briggs, 1909. *Author's collection.*

In 1913, Briggs bought the Continental Trust Company Building from Springer and Hughes but did not move Interstate's operations to it until 1918, after remodeling the banking rooms. At this time, the building acquired the name it would bear until its demolition. It was a good time to move; one of the building's marquee tenants was the Denver Branch of the Federal Reserve Bank of Kansas City, occupying an entire floor. By this time, Briggs had become socially prominent; his son Frank Jr. was a star athlete at East High School. In 1919, Denver Presbyterians acquired land on Grasshopper Hill west of City Park to build a hospital and made Briggs president and chief fundraiser of the organization formed to construct it (the hospital, now Presbyterian–St. Luke's, remains there today). In late 1922, Briggs announced his candidacy for mayor, resigning from Interstate

Trust. He established his headquarters at the Gas & Electric Building, with a "Colored Voters Headquarters" at 20th and Welton Streets. The Ku Klux Klan was then ascendant in Colorado politics, and their favored candidate, Democrat Benjamin F. Stapleton, won easily; Republican Briggs, promising a "progressive program of municipal development" along the lines of late mayor Robert W. Speer, came in fourth place in a ranked-choice vote.

The mayoral campaign served as a convenient excuse: he had not really resigned to run but because Interstate's directors, along with, *sotto voce*, the state bank commissioner, had forced him out. They had discovered irregularities serious enough to endanger the bank's future; ultimately, the commissioner stepped in and closed the bank on August 23, 1923, barely three months after the election. It was "the third bank failure to occur in the same building within thirty years," *The Post* noted. Perhaps Briggs thought if he won the mayoralty he would have escaped prosecution, but without it he was at the mercy of District Attorney Philip S. Van Cise, fresh from his famous capture of "Bunco King" Lou Blonger and his gang. Given Van Cise's crusading spirit, he likely would have prosecuted a Mayor Briggs anyway. In December, a grand jury charged Briggs with fourteen counts of embezzlement, related to "irregular dealings as far back as 1913." Damningly, he had taken stock in Colonial Oil Company deposited as loan collateral, sold it higher than it had been valued, retained the profit and repurchased shares when the price fell, to re-deposit against his customer's loan. In April 1924, he went on trial, the prosecution led by Van Cise, who called on Federal District Judge J. Foster Symes, a onetime Interstate director, as a chief witness. After "one of the slowest and most monotonous cases ever heard in the criminal court," a jury found him guilty after just seventy-six minutes of deliberation. Van Cise would be disappointed: despite his prosecution under a law meant to entail a twenty-year prison term, the judge fined Briggs just $2,000. Bonfils and Tammen's *Post*, which never allowed mere journalism to obscure righteous outrage, railed against a "ridiculous punishment…one of the most absurd judgments ever pronounced in a Colorado court." The anonymous writer, quite possibly Bonfils, continued, "Truly, Justice is blind—also deaf, dumb and paralyzed when such things as this can happen."

Yet "Justice" can have her revenge. Briggs, long a member of Union Lodge No. 7, A.F. & A.M., was drummed out of the Masons at a meeting attended by over four hundred at the Masonic Temple on Welton Street. Now a free man, Briggs reestablished himself in business if not in society. He bought oil stocks, investing in Denver-based Continental Oil Company;

the corporation even named one of its best-producing wells after him. In a twist of fate, Briggs died suddenly on February 27, 1935, at age sixty-four. He was testifying in court as an expert witness in a case unrelated to his banking past when his heart gave out; despite the presence of a doctor, he could not be revived.

After this notorious episode, the building faded from the headlines. This corner in what was then called "lower downtown" acquired a seedy air as business activities migrated southeastwardly. David May's store moved to Champa Street in 1906, and Guldman's closed in 1941. In 1958, the intersection's other anchor, the Daniels and Fisher department store, having merged with May Company, moved to 16th and Tremont Streets. Furniture stores interspersed with pawnshops and other secondary businesses filled neighboring buildings; nearby Larimer Street acquired a national reputation as a skid row. When Denver voters passed DURA's Skyline Project in 1967, the building was still in good shape. Shortly after the election, DURA issued a list of buildings within the Skyline area that were to be saved and "resold to developers for rehabilitation," including

The Interstate Trust Company Building in its later years, circa 1970. *Author's collection.*

the Daniels and Fisher Tower, Central Bank (later lost) and a handful of others. DURA considered the zone between 15th and 18th Streets as vital to the project's success and wanted to preserve as little as possible.

With the Interstate Trust Building, DURA confronted an obstacle. Its owners, Royal Judd (whose family had possessed it since the 1920s) and Lou Weinstein, envisioned cleaning it, bringing it to modern standards and reintroducing it to Denver to demonstrate the economic sense of historic preservation. DURA was unyielding: it had negotiated with Central Bank for the block, and by the time Judd and Weinstein announced their plans, DURA had already arranged to sell the block for $1,170,000 to a joint venture consisting of Central Bank, Rio Grande Industries (the Denver and Rio Grande Railroad) and Texas developer Charles H. Leavell. A new office building would stretch from 16th to 15th, facing a strip of greenery called Skyline Park, the Skyline Plan's centerpiece. To battle DURA, Judd and Weinstein hired George Creamer. His clients planned to spend between $800,000 and $1,000,000 on renovation; DURA offered them $250,000 for the land and nothing for the building, which Creamer said was worth between $600,000 and $900,000 in its un-renovated state. Taking the case to the Colorado Supreme Court, Creamer asserted that DURA's action constituted an illegal taking of private property, not for a public purpose but for "an already arranged resale…without the process of law and a deprivation of equal protection of the laws, violative [*sic*] alike of the Constitution[s] of the United States…and Colorado." Architect Alan Fisher testified to the building's soundness, architectural importance and potential for "restoration to a highly desirable office accommodation, preserving the basic interior and design of this fascinating Victorian edifice." DURA won. The building was imploded on November 14, 1970. Its replacement, the black aluminum Park Central designed by William C. Muchow, opened in 1973. Had Muchow been forced to design around a renovated Interstate Trust Company Building, the result would have been different and, probably, better.[16]

MAJESTIC AND METROPOLITAN BUILDINGS

Although lacking common architecture and ownership, two neighboring office buildings that stood on 16th Street between Cleveland and Court Places can be considered as a set. Both were the same height, both anchored 16th's upper end and the same developer demolished both. The older

The Majestic Building, circa 1913. *Denver Public Library, Western History Collection, MCC-379; photograph by Louis Charles McClure.*

Majestic Building had five sides and three fronts, thanks to its site facing three streets: 16th, Cleveland and Broadway. Eight stories high, with the first three of rusticated granite and upper floors of pressed brick, it was designed by Frank E. Edbrooke. With Corinthian pilasters and a seventh floor graced with elegant arches framing banks of windows, its façade was similar to Edbrooke's other office blocks. Architectural historian Richard Brettell felt that it was "one of Edbrooke's most confusing and fussy commercial structures" yet also "one of the most exuberant buildings constructed in Denver during the nineteenth century." For years, it was a prestigious business address.

Its builder, John Aten McMurtrie, began construction in late 1895, two years after the Panic of 1893 decimated Colorado's economy, as a statement of faith in Denver's future. The building soon reached its full height, but for reasons unknown, construction stopped before windows were installed or the interior was finished. Photographs from this period show lower floors covered by advertising billboards. McMurtrie died in

February 1899, and his estate sold the unfinished edifice for $300,000 to Dennis Sheedy and Charles B. Kountze, longtime business partners in Colorado National Bank and The Denver Dry Goods Company, who announced vague plans of housing a department store on lower floors with apartments above. In 1900, a new entity, Majestic Improvement Company, composed of partners David Halliday Moffat and Bennett and Myers Realty, bought the building and announced plans for a hotel, to be managed by Maxcy Tabor, then of The Brown Palace. Finally in 1901, work resumed, but the Majestic Building, as the partners named it, would be a simple office block. They recognized that while the Majestic was not in the heart of the business district, its location near the county courthouse, The Brown and the State Capitol made it ideal for tenants who needed to be near those places, particularly attorneys. From 1903 to 1911, Denver Tramway Company and the related Denver and Northwestern Railroad occupied three floors, including president William Gray Evans. In 1916, Evans crony Robert W. Speer opened his campaign headquarters in the

The Metropolitan Building with six stories, circa 1911. *Denver Public Library, Western History Collection, MCC-1614; photograph by Louis Charles McClure.*

The Metropolitan Building with nine stories, Majestic Building at right, circa 1916. *Denver Public Library, Western History Collection, MCC-2723; photograph by Louis Charles McClure.*

Majestic, hoping for a political comeback with a third mayoral term. The building's longest tenant was Colorado State Bank, occupying part of the ground floor from 1908 until moving across Broadway in 1971.

Across the alley, the Metropolitan Building was a project of Denver clothiers Merritt William Gano and William Day Downs, whose store thrived down 16th Street at Stout. In 1910, they engaged George Hebard Williamson, of Sterner and Williamson, for a nine-story building at 16th and Court Place specifically to house medical and dental offices. Concerned about attracting enough tenants, they at first built a six-story structure, topped by a crenelated parapet, the 16th Street façade divided by a light well. In 1915, they added three more floors, making nine, although thanks to lower ceilings the finished building's cornice line matched the eight-story Majestic Building. Lower floors were of blond brick with the topmost faced in white glazed terra cotta with French Gothic details; elaborate pinnacles above the cornice created a lively skyline, calling out to the contemporaneous French Gothic Cathedral of the Immaculate

The Majestic Building during demolition, 1977. *Thomas J. Noel collection; photograph by Thomas J. Noel.*

The Majestic Building prior to demolition, 1977. *Thomas J. Noel collection; photograph by Thomas J. Noel.*

Conception, nearby at East Colfax Avenue and Logan Street. Above the street floor, elegant crowned lanterns illuminated the sidewalk. The corner space facing Court Place housed a pharmacy for the building's entire tenure, serving patients of upstairs tenants. The initial occupant was Shaw Drug Company, later Scholz Drug Company and ultimately Walgreen's.

In the early 1970s, building contractor Nicholas R. Petry began assembling the block's properties; by 1974, he owned it completely. In 1976, developer Oxford-Ansco, a partnership between the Canadian Oxford Properties and local billionaire Philip Frederick Anschutz, bought Petry's holdings. This was the era of Denver's great, but short-lived, oil boom. Oxford-Ansco demolished the Majestic Building first, followed by the Metropolitan and other structures and in 1980 opened the mirror-glass twin towers of Great West Plaza. While one tower occupies the former Majestic Building corner, where the Metropolitan once stood a bleak wind-swept plaza fails to entice passersby to linger long enough to imagine what once stood here.[17]

MINING EXCHANGE BUILDING

"There is an air of nostalgia about the entire building, which is surrounded by modern architecture. It still has an appeal for those who are interested in having old landmarks preserved." So wrote historian Nolie Mumey in 1962. In 1963, the air of nostalgia gave way to the smell of commerce when one of Denver's finest pre-Panic buildings, just six decades old, was demolished. We have fragments: the *Old Prospector* statue, twelve feet high, stands in front of Brooks Towers, the residential building that replaced the Mining Exchange and the block's other structures; and a carved bull and bear, once gracing the building's arched entry, now gaze at passersby in the Courtyard of the Bull and Bear in Larimer Square, rescued by preservationist Dana Crawford. The building was doomed by its times: instead of perceiving it as a monument to Colorado's mineral mining heritage or as a fine example of Richardsonian Romanesque architecture with its intricate carvings, graceful curved corners and eccentric clock tower, Denver's power brokers saw only an outmoded pile standing in the way of progress.

The design was by H. William Kirchner and August Kirchner, St. Louis architects with a Denver branch office. Their client was the Colorado Mining Stock Exchange. While Colorado still boasts active mining operations in the twenty-first century, mineral extraction is not central to its economy the way it was in the nineteenth. Mine owners and investors, wealthy and powerful men, required a building that reflected their importance and would provide a "venue to facilitate the selling of stock to the investing public, a place where brokers could mix with potential investors in an exciting, sometimes electric, atmosphere," per mining historian James B. Copeland. Mining investment companies leased office space upstairs, and investors perused maps, read prospectuses and even examined ore samples in the exchange.

The Colorado Mining Stock Exchange, organized on June 18, 1889, was not Denver's first such entity, nor would it be its last; ultimately, fourteen Denver mining stock exchanges operated for some period of time. Some lasted only months, but this one lasted for ten years, and historians consider it the second-most successful mining stock exchange in Colorado, after one in Colorado Springs. Over its lifespan, more than 341,400,000 shares in 248 mining companies traded, with an aggregate value of $22,612,000. Members paid for seats on the exchange, and these were limited in number; before the Panic of 1893, 225 men held memberships, some paying as much as $500 for them. The exchange's first president was George F. Batchelder; smelter owner and banker Dennis Sheedy served as treasurer; Charles E.

The Mining Exchange Building, circa 1892. *History Colorado, 20102540; photograph by William Henry Jackson.*

Taylor succeeded Batchelder in 1891. "Silver King" Horace Tabor served on the board but was not involved in operations. Most shares traded were in Cripple Creek gold mines. In 1899, the Colorado Mining Stock Exchange dissolved and was reorganized as the Denver Stock Exchange. Its board included several of Denver's wealthiest men, such as John F. Campion (serving as president), David H. Moffat, James B. Grant and Eben Smith. It continued as a mining stock exchange for several years before dissolving.

When the building opened on November 18, 1891, the exchange had spent $450,000 on construction and land, and it showed. The first three floors were red sandstone, some pieces rusticated and others smooth. The next two floors were red pressed brick, with the sixth and seventh floors again in red sandstone. The tower's upper portion was a mixture of brick and sandstone, and the roof was of red tile. Elaborate Romanesque stone carvings enriched and enlivened the composition; four gargoyles projected from the tower's corners. Curiously, although the tower was clearly designed to include a clock on each side, none was ever installed. Crowning it all, 165 feet from the sidewalk, the *Old Prospector* was visible for miles.

This sculpture was modeled on John William Straughn (1842–1908), an Indianan and Union Civil War veteran who arrived in Colorado in the mid-1880s. He had actually prospected for gold, making him legitimately an "Old Prospector," and then operated a blacksmith shop in Black Hawk. Per Mumey, "He wore a flowing beard with long hair, and was usually attired in a long-tailed coat made of black broadcloth. He wore shiny, black boots which gave him the appearance of a southern gentleman, thus he acquired the title of 'Colonel.'" His distinctiveness made him a favorite with photographers and artists; one painting of him, *Typical Prospector*, was displayed in the Colorado Building at the 1893 Chicago World's Fair. It later hung in the Windsor Hotel's bar before disappearing. Commissioned to provide a sculpture for the tower, Alphonse Pelzer, who worked for Salem, Ohio metal fabricator W.H. Mullens, based it on a photograph of Straughn. The finished work cost $1,000. In 1938, the large nugget in his hands was plated with actual gold.

Entering through the archway, visitors passed through a marble vestibule with paneled walls and stained glass. A cast-iron stairway rose from this lobby to the second-floor trading hall, which measured fifty by seventy feet, with a thirty-foot ceiling and elaborate brass chandeliers. Visitors watched traders from third-floor galleries overlooking the floor. The hall included a telegraph station and exhibition space for mineral samples. While ground-floor storefronts hosted typical retail activities, upper floors were leased to businesses, both mining-related and not. On the seventh floor, traders enjoyed a clubroom and café. Tourists visited the building too, paying fifteen cents to view Denver from the tower. All this opulence had to be paid for, and after the Panic of 1893, the Colorado Mining Stock Exchange found itself taking second and third mortgages; in 1896,

The Mining Exchange Building entry with bull and bear carvings, 1964. *History Colorado, 10039498.*

the exchange sold the building for just $287,955, two-thirds of what it had spent to build it.

After the exchange closed, the large second-floor hall remained, sometimes rented out for dances. The Denver Mining Club maintained a small museum. The building continued as an office building with ground-floor shops. One tenant occupying the 15th and Arapahoe corner was

The Mining Stock Exchange Building trading floor, 1902. *Denver Public Library, Western History Collection, X-61444.*

View looking east from the Mining Exchange Building tower, circa 1900. *Author's collection.*

Central Savings Bank, which in 1911 moved across Arapahoe to its own nine-story tower (demolished 1990); architect Jules Jacques Benoit Benedict gave it a rounded corner, echoing the Mining Exchange's curve. After World War II, the building sold for about $200,000, and new owners tried to give it a second life by modernizing and upgrading. It was to no avail; new high-rise towers attracted most of downtown's leases, and the building gradually grew emptier. In 1962, Central Bank president Elwood Brooks looked out his windows and was not pleased. This corner of downtown had grown dowdy and rundown in his eyes. With partners including bank vice president Armand Asborno, he set up Park City Realty Corporation, its purpose to redevelop the bank's immediate vicinity. In 1962, it bought the Mining Exchange Building and others across the alley, announcing a forty-two-story high-rise apartment tower, the first such project in downtown. In August, a demolition company carefully lowered the *Old Prospector* so it could be displayed in Central Bank's lobby during the construction period. Prior to the new building's completion, Brooks died, so the tower, now condominiums, honors his name. Since 1968, the *Old Prospector*, no longer prominent on the skyline, has watched over passersby from just above the sidewalk.[18]

Republic Building

Roger Oram's collection of over eight thousand signatures to save the Republic Building at 16th and Tremont Streets resulted in a toothless city council resolution, passed unanimously, but little else. It was the winter of 1980–81, and Denver was in the middle of its largest-ever construction boom. Oil drove it; Denver needed space for hundreds of branches of Texas, Oklahoma and Alberta oil companies with their geologists and dealmakers pursuing fossil fuel riches. For several cold weeks, Oram and friends gathered signatures, listening to Denverites reminisce—everyone had stories of visiting doctors or dentists, of walking down tile-floored corridors with marble wainscoted walls, perhaps stopping in marble-partitioned restrooms. "The Republic always made me feel kind of grand," Oram told a *Rocky Mountain News* reporter. "It made you feel good just going in there. With the manually operated elevators, you always felt like you got red-carpet service even though you were a common, ordinary man." It was no ordinary man planning to demolish the building for what is still today Denver's tallest skyscraper, the fifty-six-story Republic Plaza, but a billionaire who had made his fortune in oil, Philip Anschutz. He partnered with Edmonton, Alberta–based Oxford Development Company Ltd., itself an offshoot of an oil company, in Oxford-Ansco, which remade large swaths of downtown between 1977 and 1984, demolishing not only the Republic Building but also the aforementioned Majestic and Metropolitan Buildings, the Patterson Building on 17th and Welton Streets, the Continental Oil Building on 18th and Glenarm and smaller treasures.

The Republic's demolition during that boom was one of Denver history's ironies, as it had itself been built in the mid-1920s boom that produced several elegant high-rises, most now lost. It replaced the Ohio Block, a two-story structure that was home to, among others, Yee Foo Lun, an herbalist and practitioner of traditional Chinese medicine. Its replacement was built for practitioners of western medicine, doctors and dentists, and it was initially called the Medical Arts Building; why the developers chose the name Republic is unknown, but they may have wanted a more impressive-sounding moniker. The land had long been property of downtown's largest landowner, Walter Scott Cheesman, and his estate. In 1925, Tremont Investment Company, led by realtor Roy J. Dutton, bought the eight lots from Cheesman Investment Company and began construction. Joining Dutton were H.J. Watts; Herman A. Burkhardt, of Burkhardt Steel & Iron; and the building's architect, George Meredith Musick, who took a one-quarter ownership share rather than a fee for his first large-scale commission. The steel-framed building enclosed approximately four hundred offices spread across 152,000 square feet along with fourteen ground-floor retail spaces totaling 11,000 square feet; for the building's entire fifty-five-year lifetime, a drugstore occupied the corner space, most of its prescriptions sent by doctors upstairs. Pre-leasing was already at 50 percent occupancy when construction began; by its 1927 completion, it was nearly full.

Oram was correct: this was the common man's palace. Its neo-Gothic architecture boasted abundant glazed terra-cotta detailing executed by the Denver Terra Cotta Company. Its most popular exterior features were sixteen busts of doctors and dentists mounted between the second and third floors; designed by Musick or his brother James Roger Musick, each was based on a tenant. The ornamentation at the building's crown gave it a lively silhouette. Every office had natural light, thanks to a light court, sixty-five feet across and sixty-five feet deep, facing Tremont. Every office had gas lines, compressed air, hot and cold water and AC and DC electricity—far more infrastructure than ordinary office buildings. The Republic was twelve stories high, limited by a 1908 height ordinance; the basement included a

The Republic Building, 1927. *Denver Public Library, Western History Collection, X-25126; photograph by J.H. Cook.*

126-car garage, Denver's first underground parking. Altogether, the investors spent $4.5 million on land and building.

Perhaps it was too extravagantly built. When money became tight in the Great Depression, the Cheesman Investment Company foreclosed, and investors were left with nothing. Musick was later philosophical about it,

The Republic Building, 1927; note terra-cotta busts below the second-floor cornice. *Denver Public Library, Western History Collection, X-25123; photograph by Roy Hyskell.*

writing in his autobiography, "Had not the foreclosure occurred I would have become wealthy. Looking back I believe the foreclosure was a good thing for me." Indeed, he enjoyed a long, lucrative career, designing or collaborating on scores of landmarks, many still standing. The Cheesman interests found ways to profit from their ownership—vacuum cleaner bags were not tossed away but sent to a sifting service that mined them for dentists' gold, netting up to forty dollars each month. In 1958, the Republic Building Corporation bought the remaining lots along Tremont up to 17th Street and in 1964 erected a five-hundred-car garage, the need for parking having grown beyond what was available underneath the building.

Oxford-Ansco bought the Republic Building in August 1977. Tenants continued caring for patients, not paying attention to their new landlord demolishing other buildings; some claimed later that had they known the building's fate, they might have joined together to buy it. Yet Oxford-Ansco had bought it for the express purpose of building something bigger, and in 1980, they announced plans for the sixty-story Republic Plaza; the Federal Aviation Administration, concerned about flights approaching Stapleton International Airport just five miles away, forced its shortening to fifty-six floors. When the demolition company began removing the terra-cotta busts, hundreds asked for them, but Anschutz claimed them for his Polo

Grounds house (he ultimately donated them to the Colorado Historical Society). Republic Plaza was topped off in 1983; when it opened in 1984, hardly anyone occupied it, Denver's economy having fallen into a funk with the oil price crash. For years, critics derided it as a "see-through" building because dozens of floors sat empty in such a contrast to the Republic Building's usually full occupancy from the time it opened to its last year of existence.[19]

Tabor Grand Opera House

More than any other vanished landmark, the Tabor Grand, on the western corner of 16th and Curtis Streets, has captivated imaginations of generations of Denverites. Its 1964 demolition by Park City Realty (not by DURA, as many misremember) brought tears but no protests because many believed that Denver needed to shed its hoary past. If there is a silver lining to its loss it is that 1964 also saw the birth of Denver's modern preservation movement when Dana Crawford began buying buildings to create Larimer Square. Soon others, missing the Tabor Grand, the Windsor Hotel and so many grand mansions, coalesced around saving what pieces remained of Denver's glorious, silver-built legacy.

Horace Tabor had already built one opera house on Leadville's Harrison Avenue when, in 1880, he announced a magnificent venue for Denver. His recently completed Tabor Block, Denver's finest office building, stood three blocks northwest at 16th and Larimer, and like that edifice, the Tabor Grand Opera House was five stories high. Its designer was Chicago's Willoughby James Edbrooke, whose brother Frank came to supervise construction (and would shortly become Denver's most prominent commercial architect). In addition to the ornate auditorium, the Opera House Block had office space upstairs, ground-floor shops and the well-stocked Opera House Bar, a personal project of Tabor's that was outfitted with marble floors, chandeliers, stained glass and tropical plants, complementing a thirty-two-foot solid marble bar.

The *Rocky Mountain News* described the architecture as "an enriched adaptation of the prevailing 'Queen Anne,'" and upon completion, the red pressed brick, mansard-roofed building presented a lively skyline, with a prominent corner tower on 16th, a secondary tower at the southwestern end and fifth-floor dormers (later squared off when the fifth was converted to a regular floor). Gray granite columns framed the 16th Street main entrance;

a secondary entrance opened to Curtis Street. Inside, the L-shaped lobby was carpeted in crimson bordered by green and lit by gas chandeliers, with dark, polished cherry woodwork. The auditorium, seventy-one feet wide by ninety deep, was similarly deluxe, outfitted in a style Edbrooke termed "modified Egyptian Moresque." The 1,500 seats were arranged in three tiers, with tapestry-lined formal boxes flanking the stage (Box A was for Tabor's exclusive use). A cut crystal chandelier hung from a shallow ceiling dome. Above the proscenium, a mural by Robert Hopkins illustrated *Hector's Adieu to Andromache*, and the artist's painted drop curtain portrayed romantic architectural ruins. Below, he painted poet Charles Kingsley's words that foretold Tabor's future, had the millionaire but guessed: "So fleet the works of men, back to their earth again; Ancient and holy things fade like a dream."[20] Upholstery, carpeting and furniture came from Chicago's Marshall Field & Company. Altogether, Tabor expended $850,000 on his jewel.

Opening night, September 5, 1881, saw Denver society turn out to hear diva Emma Abbott, one of the era's best-known sopranos, perform the "mad scene" from Donzietti's *Lucia di Lammermoor* prior to a full performance of William Vincent Wallace's then-popular opera *Maritana*. Tabor was there,

Opposite: The Tabor Grand Opera House, circa 1892. *History Colorado, 20102548; photograph by William Henry Jackson.*

Above: The Tabor Grand Opera House auditorium, 1881. *Denver Public Library, Western History Collection, X-24748; photograph by Joseph Collier.*

of course, giving a speech and presented with an autographed album and gold watch fob paid for by public subscription. Not present was his estranged wife, Augusta, who had entreated with Horace in a letter two days earlier to let her attend the opening "and witness the Glory that you are to receive." She promised to "humble myself in the dust at your feet if you will only return." Present in the audience, but not in the Tabor box, was his future wife, Elizabeth Bonduel McCourt Doe ("Baby Doe").

It was built for Denver's people, and the people came. It showed profits almost immediately, particularly once Tabor's brother-in-law Peter McCourt took over management after Tabor quarreled with business partner William Bush. McCourt's "Silver Circuit" brought eastern acts whose trip west was made profitable by his ability to book them into not only the Tabor but also smaller theaters across Colorado, Utah and Wyoming. The fare was not exclusively operatic: *Uncle Tom's Cabin* was perennially popular, as were Shakespeare's plays. The era's great actors appeared, including Lawrence Barrett, Helena Modjeska, Sarah Bernhardt, Eddie Foy, Edwin Booth and Jack Langrishe, the "Father of Colorado Theater." Not everyone was fully welcome, however. James Hawkins, a Black man, sued Tabor after ushers would not honor his parquet-level tickets; Black people were allowed in nosebleed seats upstairs but not on the more visible parquet. Another African American, James Mackey, sued on similar grounds after being ejected by the police; the case went to the Colorado Supreme Court, where it was dismissed.

Tabor lost the Opera House in 1896, defaulting on a mortgage he had taken out to fund other parts of his crumbling empire. By this time, the Broadway Theatre uptown had eclipsed the Tabor in size and social cachet. In 1897, McCourt, who ran the Broadway, regained management of the Tabor, giving him flexibility to book more prestigious shows uptown and popular, but sometimes second-rate, shows at the Tabor. The grand palace came to be surrounded by smaller theaters, most with elaborate fronts outlined in white light bulbs, and by the 1910s, Curtis Street from 15th to 18th Streets was Denver's primary entertainment district. These other venues booked vaudeville acts and movies; the Tabor screened its first film in 1906, a documentary on the San Francisco earthquake and fire. In 1915, it showed D.W. Griffith's racist epic, *The Birth of a Nation*.

In 1921, investors bought the forty-year-old Tabor and closed it for remodeling by Denver architects William Ellsworth Fisher and Arthur Addison Fisher. When it reopened, it was called the Colorado Theater. Gone were the boxes and cherrywood trimmings. Accommodating three thousand on two levels, the auditorium now boasted a Spanish Renaissance interior, a

The Tabor Theater auditorium, circa 1922, after the Fisher and Fisher remodeling. *Denver Public Library, Western History Collection, X-24753, photograph by Colorado Photo Company.*

spectacularly ornamented coved ceiling and curved walls. In 1929, Denver movie impresario Harry E. Huffman took over, wisely restoring the nostalgic Tabor name. He added live entertainment, creating the Taborettes line of chorus girls, modeled on Radio City's Rockettes. He booked new stars like Donald O'Conner, the Andrews Sisters and the Gumm Sisters (Mary Jane, Dorothy Virginia and Frances Ethel, better remembered as Judy Garland). Movies were the main draw, and Hoffman later turned over management to the Fox-Intermountain circuit. After World War II, the Tabor hosted a few prestigious first-run films, including *Oklahoma!*, but increasingly relied on second-run and B-movies. In 1955, the city-owned Auditorium Theater at 14th and Curtis closed for remodeling, so traveling Broadway shows such as *Kismet* and *Teahouse of the August Moon* briefly lit the Tabor's marquee. In its final years, it screened predominantly Spanish-language movies to Denver's growing Hispanic population.

By this time, there was growing consensus among Denver's white business community that "lower downtown," as the area northwest of Curtis Street was called, needed shaking up. As described previously, Central Bank and

Park City Realty began "cleaning up" adjacent blocks through demolition and new construction. After the Mining Exchange, it set its sights on the block diagonally opposite the bank, home to the Tabor and the old Post Office and Customs House (another indirect Tabor legacy). It acquired the Tabor in early 1963 and demolished it in 1964, announcing more high-rise apartment towers. Park City scrapped these plans, however, when the Denver Branch of the Federal Reserve Bank of Kansas City, then in cramped quarters at 17th and Arapahoe Streets, threatened to move to the suburbs. Downtown banks abhorred the idea, so Park City rapidly made a deal with the Fed, resulting in the Brutalist-style bank that occupies the block today.[21]

Chapter 3

RETAIL LANDMARKS

Appel & Company

When men and boys' clothier Appel & Company hired Frank Edbrooke to design a new four-story, forty-seven-thousand-square-foot emporium on the southern corner of 16th and Larimer Streets in 1892, it was running counter to the general trend. Larimer had long been an important street, but Denver's trade was moving steadily up 16th away from it. The Appel family had been immensely successful, however, and believed in Larimer. Patriarch Simon Appel had founded the store in 1869 as Star Clothing House, on Blake Street between 14th and 15th Streets. Business grew rapidly; in 1875, it moved to the Blake and 15th corner, and in 1876, Appel changed the name to S. Appel, Son & Company. After bringing all three sons—Moses S., Israel M. and Jacob S. Appel—into the firm, he retired. In 1883, Appel & Company moved into a two-story building at 16th and Larimer. It came down in 1891 to build the magnificent new one that opened in July 1892.

Edbrooke's design, while utilizing traditional elements, anticipated modernism with its repetitive façade. It featured a "framework of steel independent of the walls," per a grand opening advertisement, and the latest conveniences, including gas and electric lighting and a "richly upholstered" elevator fitted with "handsome beveled mirrors" and "all the modern safety clutches and air cushion, making accidents an impossibility." Huge plate-glass windows were lined with mirrors, as were upstairs windows, to reflect light into the interior. Street-level floors were tiled, with oiled hard rock maple floors upstairs. Patrons purchased shoes, hats and furnishings at street

The Appel & Company Building, circa 1892. *Author's collection.*

level, ascending to the second for a complete men's clothing department. The third floor housed boys' departments and merchant-tailoring with the "best trained cutters in Denver"—the store employed upward of fifty tailors for custom suits, pants and shirts—while the fourth housed shipping and receiving. The basement, in addition to Edison electric dynamos, had luggage, rubber goods and miners' equipment departments. The July 6 grand opening, attended by twenty-five thousand, began with a morning parade of employees and continued with luncheon for the governor and business leaders, an afternoon reception for ladies and children and an evening dedication ceremony and public reception, followed by fireworks launched from the rooftop. Bands and orchestras entertained visitors.

One year later, the Panic of 1893 hit, but Appel survived; by 1896, it had renamed itself Appel's Big Store, and newspaper advertising proclaimed it "the People's Store." In 1899, however, the indebted brothers lost it to banker George E. Ross-Lewin, First National's vice president, who liquidated it. In September 1900, the building reopened as a full-line department store including ladies' departments, calling itself the People's Big Store. Denver's ladies weren't having it. Moses Appel still owned the premises, and in January 1902, his lawyers forced People's to vacate. The building was repurposed

The Appel Building, renamed the Barnett Building, on fire, February 17, 1932. *Denver Public Library, Western History Collection, Rh-1452; photograph by Harry Mellon Rhoads.*

with offices upstairs and shops below. A 1932 fire destroyed upper floors; the top two were removed and the two remaining floors were modernized. The building came down during the Skyline Project, and Writer Square occupies the block today.[22]

The Appel story did not end in 1899. That year, Jacob Appel moved uptown to 720 16th Street, occupying space recently vacated by Knight-Campbell Music Company in the Mack Block at California, diagonally opposite The Denver Dry Goods, one of downtown's best corners. J.S. Appel's Store, as he named it, sold "women's apparel exclusively." By all accounts, it succeeded for a time, yet Appel had to liquidate to pay creditors at the beginning of 1907. Finding new investors, he regrouped and reopened and by the beginning of 1911 was planning to expand. By November, it had unraveled. In bankruptcy court, it emerged that Appel's attorney, Alfred Muller, had deceived backers, including *Rocky Mountain News* owner Thomas Patterson, National Jewish Hospital and a New York company. Muller committed suicide, and Appel was ruined. He blamed his collapse on Dun & Bradstreet's poor credit rating but later admitted to kiting checks with Muller; creditors demanded he be charged with fraud. In 1912, his brother-in-law bought the store's assets and opened Imperial Suit and Cloak Company, with Appel actually running it, but this final incarnation of what had begun in 1869 as Star Clothing House failed several months later, with creditors liquidating its inventory.[23]

Cottrell's

Decades after its namesake business closed, "Cottrell's, the mans store" signage graced the second floor of a rundown-looking building at 16th and Welton Streets. Many of its customers had retired or died by the time it came down in 2020, but for nearly a century, Cottrell's reigned as a leading menswear shop. George F. Cottrell ("COTT-rul") came to Denver from Providence, Rhode Island, in 1890 at age twenty-seven, seeking relief from chronic hay fever. A clothing salesman with fifteen years' experience, he found work at a Larimer Street emporium that sent him traveling through mountain towns. In Leadville, he encountered a "noted mining man" who wanted silk shirts. Cottrell, when asked the price, told him twenty-five dollars, and the wealthy miner bought two—when their price in Providence was only one dollar. His employer kept him on.

On Friday, July 23, 1893, walking up 16th Street, Cottrell encountered a bankrupt men's store between California and Welton Streets. July was the peak of the 1893 Panic; stores were desperate for cash. On this same day, four banks failed; that summer, more than half of Denver's banks closed. Cottrell saw opportunity: Daniels and Fisher department store, the shop's major creditor, had taken over and was selling stock and fixtures for $750 in cash. Cottrell negotiated with the manager, reducing that to $675, and went to his bank to withdraw funds. The bank said he could have it after a ninety-day wait, so he went to the wealthiest man he knew, flour millionaire John Kernan Mullen, and explained his predicament. Mullen took him to visit William Garrett Fisher at his store. Fisher would not sell the shop on a promise of future cash but accepted Mullen's "personal note," and Cottrell Clothing Company was born.

Denver's wealthy became regular patrons, with Cottrell selling suits and hats to Henry Cordes Brown, Senator Henry Moore Teller and Senator Thomas Patterson. Yet he also catered to humbler types; in 1936, he told the *Colorado Labor Advocate* he "attribute[d] a large part of his success to the support of union men." The shop, enlarged several times, remained in the Crandall Block at 16th and Welton Streets until a 1912 fire; it reopened in the Mack Block across the alley. Cottrell died in 1938, and his widow, along with longtime employees H.A. Rodecker and William E. Glass, kept Cottrell's going. In 1948, anticipating Denver's growth and needing to vacate the scheduled-for-demolition Mack Block, Rodecker and Glass signed a lease in the Liebhardt Building, a two-story structure built in 1915 in place of the burned Crandall Block. When the new Cottrell's opened in 1950, it occupied all of the fully remodeled, twenty-eight-thousand-square-foot structure, now with an elegant Modernist façade of dark Virginia greenstone trimmed with aluminum. The street level featured showcase windows for passersby, while large second-floor windows allowed ample light to illuminate Cottrell's vast suit selection. The interior had a masculine, clubby feeling, with tan and brown on the first floor and green on the second, with light oak fixtures. Escalators connected the floors, and over eighty employees assisted customers. The grand opening's guest of honor was octogenarian Frank Carruthers, retired advertising manager for *The Denver Post*, who, hearing of Cottrell's Mullen connection, had not only sold Cottrell his first advertisement in 1893 but had also been his first customer.

Cottrell's, the mans store, circa 1990. *Denver Public Library, Western History Collection, Z-10468; photograph by Roger Whitacre.*

In the 1960s, Colorado School of Mines seniors regularly trekked from Golden to buy "Senior Stetsons," hats that only that class was allowed to wear. Although there were other Stetson dealers, Cottrell's advertised in Mines' student newspaper, informing seniors that any hat bought at Cottrell's would be "permanently hand-creased and blocked by Cottrell's expert hatters" and that it sold a complete size range, from "6-1/2 to 8 in regular, long and wide ovals." Cottrell's knew that many Mines graduates would find jobs working in downtown Denver oil and gas companies and offered all seniors free hat cleaning.

Cottrell's remained family-owned, with George's daughter Jane and his grandchildren retaining control. In 1965, it expanded to Boulder, buying Reinert Clothing Company, and it opened stores in Golden in 1968 and Southglenn Mall in 1974. In 1986, heirs sold Cottrell's to Los Angeles–based Desmond's, which retained the Cottrell's name. In 1995, ownership decided to close the Denver store, citing the rise of casual clothing—Cottrell's old-fashioned suits just weren't moving anymore. A souvenir shop, Only In Colorado, moved into the space; while it removed the Cottrell's signage on 16th Street, the Welton Street sign remained up, reminding older Denverites of former times.[24]

DAVIS & SHAW

Department stores had always sold furniture, but after Denver recovered from the 1893 Panic, independent furniture stores blossomed. Housing boomed after 1900, and homebuyers needed furnishings. Many retailers found lower downtown attractive, easily accessible but just far enough from the retail heart that rents were much lower. That these companies naturally clustered together made it simple for shoppers to compare quality and price. One of the longest-lived stores founded then was Davis & Shaw, opening its doors in 1900 at 1454 Larimer Street, in a two-story building with arched plate-glass windows, long since demolished. Senior partner Frederick Franklin Davis, from Council Bluffs, Iowa, had been a traveling furniture salesman; twenty-one years old and ambitious, he was broad-faced and clean-shaven with a cleft chin. Joining him was an older, bearded Englishman, Peter William Shaw, born in Birmingham in 1855 and resident in Denver since 1882; he had previously managed a bed store. A third partner, hardware jobber and Davis's brother-in-law Richard Ellsworth Pate, did not have his name above the door, but his descendants would own Davis & Shaw until the end. Thanks to the partners' skills and energy, the store expanded several times in its early years, leasing adjacent spaces on Larimer and knocking through the wall of the adjacent Granite Building to occupy part of its first floor. Before the store could celebrate its tenth birthday, Davis needed even more space and leased the entire six-floor Pioneer Building diagonally across 15th and Larimer.

Compared to other pre-Panic buildings, the neoclassical Pioneer Building, built by Charles B. Patterson in 1888–89, was not spectacular, but it radiated dignity, with a cut stone façade, regularly spaced windows and a simple cornice topped with balustrade and small triangular pediment—no towers, grand Richardsonian arches or decorative gewgaws. However, the 1910s mania for electric signs, combined with Davis's promotional flair, turned the Pioneer Building into an instant landmark when he installed a roof-mounted sign so tall—almost three stories high—that it soared past the Pioneer's neighbor, the eight-story Railroad Building, making "Davis & Shaw" visible day and night from a mile away. The first version featured an "electric fountain effect" utilizing hundreds of tiny light bulbs. Davis replaced it two years later with a "skyrocket" sign and then with the silhouette of a "mysterious lady in a Davis & Shaw rocking chair" amidst a flower-bedecked trellis, gazing at a crescent moon. Davis boastfully proclaimed it "one of the stellar attractions of Denver." In a 1914 advertisement for the Denver Gas and Electric Light Company, he estimated that "about 125,000 people…see or discuss our sign every night."

Regardless of whether people actually discussed Davis & Shaw's sign over the dinner table, Davis, Shaw and Pate saw business increase every year. Although in later decades the store cultivated a higher-end reputation, in its early years it catered to all classes, with varying price points—but also with a strict "one-price" policy, whether the buyer paid cash or in installments. Shoppers could trade in old furniture, and the store's workshop, in a warehouse near the 14th Street viaduct, reconditioned it for resale to less affluent buyers.

Davis, as the firm's face, became known for business acumen and for his civic activities and social prominence. In 1910, he co-founded the Larimer Street Improvement Association; his store hosted the organizational meeting. Members recognized that Larimer had lost its luster to the numbered streets, with 17th now "Wall Street of the West," 16th boasting the best stores and 15th, with its transit functions and bargain stores, sapping business from what had been Denver's "main street" in the 1870s and 1880s. Not only was Larimer unfashionable, but despite the human, streetcar and (now) automobile traffic

The Davis & Shaw Furniture Company in the Pioneer Building, circa 1916. *Denver Public Library, Western History Collection, MCC-3623; photograph by Louis Charles McClure.*

it saw, it had lost its identity. The association attempted to change that, with cleaned-up buildings, better traffic connections, more frequent streetcars and, most crucially, brighter lighting, on par with 15th, 16th and 17th, where the Robert Speer administration had installed elegant lampposts. By 1911, new arc lights illuminated Larimer from 14th to 17th. Ultimately, Larimer declined into Denver's "skid row," but not for want of Davis's efforts to keep it viable; he remained bullish on Larimer Street to the end of his life.

In 1922, Peter Shaw collapsed near his home at 611 Downing Street, dying of heart disease. Two years later, Davis sold out to Richard Pate, who became sole owner of Davis & Shaw. Davis planned to sell stoves, collaborating with "eastern interests" on a projected chain, the Universal Store Company. He opened a Denver location at 1521 Arapahoe Street, but after his wife Ingrid died in 1926, he realized his first love, furniture, was his true calling. Previously, he had purchased a 5/24 interest in the Pioneer Building; he now bought Pate's 5/24 share. Later, he bought the remaining 14/24 from its out-of-town owners, attorney Frederic Stimson and Supreme Court associate justice Louis D. Brandeis, who had purchased it years previously to settle an estate. Davis covered the "Pioneer Building" name carved below the cornice with a sign designating it the "Fred Davis Building." Pate agreed to move Davis & Shaw out within six months, and in 1927, Davis opened the Fred Davis Furniture Company.

In daily newspaper advertisements, he adopted old Davis & Shaw slogans, "Out of the High Rent District" and "Not in the High Price Clique," and added a third one, "The Store with the Orange Front." He arranged the store much as Davis & Shaw had been, with the ground floor devoted to living rooms; the mezzanine home to occasional pieces, radios and phonographs; and the second floor housing carpeting, rugs, linoleum, drapery, bedding and vacuum cleaners. On three, shoppers found bedroom furniture, including Rome and Simmons mattresses, along with chests, rockers, day beds, baby carriages and cribs. The fourth floor was devoted to dining rooms, outdoor furniture and unpainted furniture. Children's furniture filled the fifth floor: high chairs, juvenile furniture, velocipedes, wagons and toy automobiles. In the basement were Universal stoves, washing machines, kitchen cabinets and dinnerware. In 1930, even with the Depression ravaging the economy, Davis expanded into the building next door on 15th. In 1937, he modernized the street-level façade with orange, red and black glass, aluminum trim and terrazzo sidewalk. Davis's second act also included a second wife, Katherine, and a 1926 move from a nice home at 944 Lafayette Street to a grand Mediterranean-style mansion he commissioned at 140 Race Street. The Davises, including Esther (Fred and Ingrid's adult daughter), were fixtures at the club; Esther married Teller Ammons, and when he was elected Colorado's twenty-eighth governor (serving 1937–39), she became first lady.

View northeast on Champa Street from 14th Street, 1957, with Davis & Shaw visible on the right. *Thomas J. Noel collection.*

What of Davis & Shaw? Richard Pate bought property at 1434 Champa Street, opposite the Denver Gas & Electric Building, commissioning William E. and Arthur A. Fisher for a new four-story building that opened in 1927. The architects chose Greek Revival, with a terra-cotta tile façade, a twenty-eight-foot-deep recessed entry lined with show windows and a graceful curving sidewalk canopy, beckoning window shoppers to linger. If the new store was smaller than in its former home (the grand opening advertisement called it "neither mammoth nor palatial"), it exuded more elegance. Its location on a respectable street rather than increasingly shabby Larimer attracted well-heeled customers. The grand opening advertisement described it as having been founded in 1899 (not 1900) by "R.E. Pate and the late P.W. Shaw," making no mention of Fred Davis, but the Davis name remained regardless.

Fred Davis continued operating his eponymous store until June 1960, when he closed it and donated the Pioneer Building to the University of Denver (appropriate, considering the school's "Pioneers" athletic teams). He died in October. The Pioneer Building was demolished along with the rest of the half-block between the alley and Larimer as part of DURA's

Skyline Project. Davis & Shaw, later led by Richard Pate Jr. and finally Jon and Cindy Pate Jessop, operated on Champa Street until 2005. Developer Randy Nichols bought the property and adjacent ones to build the Spire, a residential tower. Despite its association with Fisher and Fisher, there was no outcry to save the Davis & Shaw Building.[25]

Fontius Shoes

Thirty-three-year-old John Jacob Fontius ("FON-shus"), newly arrived from Cleveland during the Panic summer of 1893, came to Colorado for his health. He clearly possessed unbounded optimism, as he, like George Cottrell, established his business when Denver's fortunes were at their lowest ebb. Fontius Shoe Company lore maintained that it was founded that memorably dire year, but it is likelier that it began in 1894, when May newspaper advertisements heralded the grand opening of "John J. Fontius's New Shoe Store." He found an ideal spot at 920 16th Street. This was the space closest to the alley in the Tritch Building, largely, but not yet entirely, occupied by Joslin Dry Goods. Two years later, he decamped across the alley to 900–4 16th on the Champa Street corner, and in 1906, seeking still larger quarters, he moved across Champa, occupying much of the brand-new Symes Building's ground floor.

In the 1920s, Denver boomed, and retailers grew with it. In 1923, Fontius acquired the southern corner of 16th and Welton Streets, building a two-story retail structure, Fontius Shoe Company occupying the corner and basement, with additional storefronts providing rental income. This was uptown from the department stores but still saw heavy pedestrian traffic, particularly after the Denver Theater opened next door in 1927. When John Fontius died in 1940, his shop was one of Denver's leading shoe emporiums for women, men and children. His son Harry E. Fontius led it until his 1962 death. Under Harry's leadership, Fontius opened branches, ultimately boasting eight locations.

In 1965, Harry E. Fontius Jr. felt the downtown flagship was too small, moving it a fifth and final time to a four-story building just across Welton. This had been built in 1922 for Steel's, a Buffalo, New York–based chain that failed in 1923; subsequently, it had housed a competitor, Feltman & Curme Shoes, and was now home to Dave Cook Sporting Goods, Dupler's Furs and other tenants. Fontius leased the street-level corner space and the upper floors, more than thirty-nine thousand square feet. The ground floor

Fontius Shoes, 16th and Welton Streets, 1947. *History Colorado, F-42440.*

sold men's and women's shoes, including "hard-to-find sizes over 10." On two were women's casuals, children's, slippers, hosiery and handbags, shoe repair and some clothing items. The third floor was primarily a stock room, along with a self-service bargain outlet; executive offices occupied the fourth. Fontius estimated that his family store (his sons Harry III and Marshall G. Fontius aided him) was the third-largest shoe store in the United States, after San Francisco's Sommer & Koffman and Seattle's Nordstrom.

In 1984, the family sold the company to Richard L. Gooding (president of Denver's Pepsi-Cola Bottling Company), with Marshall Fontius remaining as president, and in 1986, Gooding sold to an Arizona-based chain owned by a British shoe retailer. The Arizona concern promised to "restore its reputation for stocking hard-to-find sizes," but they bought at the worst possible time: Denver's economy was in a tailspin. Perhaps it was not as bad as 1893, but within a few years, the Fontius name was gone for good.

Except it wasn't. While Fontius's suburban mall stores were soon leased to new tenants, the old Steel's building slowly deteriorated, its tenants closing one by one, the upstairs vacant. The Fontius signage remained, and even as 16th Street slowly revived, the name "Fontius" began to symbolize decay to a generation of Denverites unfamiliar with Fontius's long history. No one remembered Steel's by the early 2000s, so the "Fontius Building" became the structure's *de facto* name. In 2007–9, developer Evan Makovsky restored the Greek Revival building (designed by Merrill Hoyt) into one of 16th Street's most distinctive, and the Fontius Building has been rechristened for its tenant, Sage Hospitality. The 1923 Fontius Building across Welton was demolished in the early 1980s for a never-built enclosed mall called Centerstone, ultimately resulting in the Denver Pavilions complex. Two earlier homes, the Tritch and Symes Buildings, remain standing; a national shoe chain occupies Fontius's space in the latter.[26]

Hedgcock & Jones

Hedgcock & Jones's story shows how changing fashions can spell doom for an industry. Englishman Frederick William Hedgcock and Herbert C. Jones came to Denver separately in 1886, both becoming clerks at Daniels and Fisher's linen and lace department. Later, they came to be relatives when Jones married Hedgcock's sister Alice. After rising to buyer positions, with frequent European sourcing trips, they left the department store in 1904 to open their own specialty shop. Two years earlier, Colorado Dry Goods Company had failed, vacating the Colorado Building at 16th and California. The men leased part of the ground floor, at 717–19 16th Street, adopted a spinning wheel as their symbol and inaugurated their business on November 16. Crowded shelves held laces of all sorts: for household use, including elaborate cutwork tablecloths, and for clothing. Denver women took pride in their fussy wardrobes, and there was endless demand for materials, including lace, to construct them. Hedgcock & Jones took off, known for its vast selection and attentive service.

Prohibition and World War I upended American life, and fashions evolved. By the early 1920s, facing increased rent but not yet recognizing that demand for their offerings would not continue growing, Hedgcock and Jones moved farther up 16th Street, midblock between Welton Street and Glenarm Place. Their new three-level emporium transformed the Brasie Block, formerly home to a bakery and furnished rooms, with an elegant neoclassical façade with large windows. Above a pair of arched third-story windows, round medallions embossed with superimposed letters *H* and *J* sheltered under gracefully curving cornices. Mannequins displaying Jazz Age fashions graced first-floor display windows, and large second-floor ones beckoned to shoppers across the street; the second floor was devoted entirely to apparel. This new version of Hedgcock-Jones (the ampersand removed), with its ground-floor emphasis on items fewer

Hedgcock-Jones in the former Brasie Block, 16th Street between Welton Street and Glenarm Place, circa 1922. *Denver Public Library, Western History Collection, X-24112.*

Denver women wanted, failed to draw crowds. Just before Christmas 1924, the partners faced reality, closing their business. Leopold Guldman bought the inventory, moved it to his Golden Eagle bargain department store at 16th and Lawrence and sold it for pennies on the dollar. Daniels and Fisher rehired Hedgcock and Jones, advertising their return. In 1927, Publix Theatres leased the left-hand half of the former Hedgcock-Jones, remodeling it into the entrance to its Denver Theatre, with the right-hand half leased to Mrs. Stover's Bungalow Candies. That cinema, along with the former Brasie Block/Hedgcock-Jones, was demolished in 1980, after a 1954 modernization had altered it beyond recognition.[27]

Knight-Campbell Music Company

Prior to commercial radio broadcasting's birth in the 1920s, no middle-class home was complete without a musical instrument for in-home entertainment. In Denver, no music store was longer-lived than Knight-Campbell, which was, for many years, also the largest. Pianos were its mainstay, but it also sold player pianos, organs, guitars and orchestral instruments, along with sheet music. In the twentieth century, it added music boxes, record players, radios and appliances. Knight-Campbell opened stores all over Colorado (Boulder, Colorado Springs, Cripple Creek, Leadville, Pueblo, Trinidad) and in Cheyenne, Wyoming. Traveling salesmen extended Knight-Campbell's reach even farther, hawking instruments in small towns across the West. It held exclusive Colorado rights to Steinway pianos and sold instruments of all qualities, from cheap to concert level. It furnished instruments to the Denver Post Boys Band and George Olinger's Highlander Boys, as well as generations of Denver children playing in school orchestras.

Founder William W. Knight, a Michigander from Battle Creek, arrived in Denver in 1873, coming west for his wife's health; his brother Frank A. Knight came too. In 1874, they partnered with Asahel K. Clark in a Howe Sewing Machine distributorship, Knight, Clark and Company. They added a musical instruments sideline in 1876, and this business grew so large that it became their primary focus. In 1879, Clark sold his share to W.W. Waterbury, creating Knight Brothers & Waterbury. In 1885, it merged with rival (Asahel K.) Clark & (Charles Y.) McClure and became Knight & McClure Music Company, with premises at 413–15 Lawrence Street (old address system: between 16th and 17th Streets). As the firm grew, the Knights rose to social prominence. In 1887, William cemented his leadership in Denver's musical life by being elected president of the Oratorio Society, a one-hundred-voice chorus that performed at the First Baptist Church. In 1891, William sold out to his partners; he would later found two other piano stores, both with Knight in their names. The original firm changed its moniker one last time, to Knight-Campbell.

George Horace Campbell, originally from Rockford, Illinois, had been in the music business his entire adult life, selling sheet music, tuning pianos and selling them. He joined Knight Brothers & Waterbury in 1880 and had been Knight & McClure's general manager since 1888. With the name change came relocation uptown, to the new Mack Block at 16th and California Streets, in the prime corner spot, diagonally opposite McNamara Dry Goods Company, with tall plate-glass windows exposing their wares to passersby.

The Paris Building, home to the Knight-Campbell Music Company, circa 1913. *Denver Public Library, Western History Collection, X-18758.*

Knight-Campbell survived the Panic of 1893 and, like other merchants, spent several years recovering, but by 1903, what had once seemed spacious was now cramped. Fortunately, a solution was nearby.

The now-forgotten Paris Building, five stories tall and designed by John J. Huddart, arose in 1891 on the opposite side of California between 16th

and 17th. This was the sort of mid-block building that once created lively streetscapes on downtown's long blocks between the numbered streets. Huddart treated each floor differently, although the overall composition appeared unified. The street level was trimmed in rusticated granite framing large windows, with red brick upper floors. Brickwork diamonds decorated spandrels between the third and fourth floors, and eyebrow moldings outlined arched fourth-floor windows. Top-floor windows were narrow, arched and unevenly spaced; the cornice was mostly brick rather than metal. The building's one-hundred-foot width allowed for two large ground-floor spaces, and Douglas Crockery Company had just vacated the left-hand one, at 1625–31 California.

In moved Knight-Campbell, occupying the street-level and upper floors, linked by an elevator. The store installed an elaborate electric sign, spanning the second and third floors, with its knight and camel ("Campbell") insignias outlined in tiny white bulbs. The firm engaged architects Aaron Gove and Thomas Walsh for the interior. Knight-Campbell promoted its new thirty-thousand-square-foot home as a "Palace of Music for Denver" and promised the "best acoustic properties" for shoppers to accurately judge instruments' tonal qualities. Performing artists gave concerts in a recital hall, and a dozen "beautifully decorated piano parlors" simulated customers' own homes. Wall cartouches featured classical composers' names, elevating Denver's taste level.

George Horace Campbell died in 1909, and his son Clarence George Campbell assumed the presidency. Frank A. Knight, still a stockholder, died in an Indiana automobile accident in 1925; he had moved east in 1904 to establish a piano factory. His brother William had preceded him in death in 1917. Yet the Knight-Campbell story is about more than just its namesakes. Charles E. Wells was a star organ salesman. Fred H. Meunier worked closely with Wells. Beginning as an elevator boy in about 1907, machinery fascinated Wells, and he gravitated naturally to pipe organs, becoming the store's primary installation specialist; in 1911, he installed an organ at Denver's leading Jewish congregation, Temple Emanuel. In 1919, Wells left to start Charles E. Wells Music Company. He took Meunier with him, along with several salesmen, tuners and others, leasing a storefront directly across California from Knight-Campbell, at 1626. Meunier left Wells after two years, becoming an independent organ installer; in 1938, he installed the massive Platt Rogers Memorial Organ at Denver's St. John's Cathedral.

The Great Depression's onset did not seem to bother Clarence Campbell, although the 1930s would see Knight-Campbell's fall from its position as

The parlor-like interior of the Knight-Campbell Music Company, circa 1913. *Denver Public Library, Western History Collection, MCC-4049; photograph by Louis Charles McClure.*

Colorado's leading music dealer and nearly close permanently. An observer would not notice the erosion, as Knight-Campbell continued paying dividends to preferred shareholders. A 1931 announcement revealed declining sales, couched in optimism: "Total sales volume in the first six months of 1931 is within 7 per cent of sales in 1930 for the same period" (meaning: sales *were down* by 7 percent). This was despite Campbell's purchase in early 1930 of rival Denver Music Company, a $2 million merger. Knight-Campbell built sales in myriad ways, including partnering with *The Denver Post* in the newspaper's musical ensembles for children. The Just Kids Orchestra was open to any child, regardless of ability or experience, and the paper avidly publicized the group's activities. Each Saturday, anyone could try out in Knight-Campbell's auditorium; presumably, parents would then patronize the store for instruments and sheet music. Knight-Campbell established a practice room for the kids in a vacant storefront next door at 1617. This was the Feldhauser Building, which Clarence had bought as an investment in 1919. *The Post* also sponsored a two-hundred-member harmonica band and a small xylophone band, both of which also practiced at Knight-Campbell.

Shareholders were dissatisfied. In early 1933, Clarence Campbell placed an advertisement regarding a suit filed by preferred stockholders against common stockholders (the largest of whom was Campbell), asserting that Knight-Campbell's financial position was sound. The fight continued through 1933, and in December, a judge placed Knight-Campbell in receivership, now controlled by preferred stockholders. Campbell appealed to the Colorado Supreme Court to retain control but by May 1934 had lost to the receivers, Albert Giesecke and Eward F. Bishop. The new men immediately closed all of Knight-Campbell's branches and moved the inventory to Denver for liquidation. Once this was sold down, Giesecke and Bishop petitioned the court to liquidate the flagship store, as they did not feel it could continue as a going concern, and it appeared they would succeed—even *The Post* stopped holding tryouts and rehearsals at Knight-Campbell, lest children encounter locked doors. Clarence Campbell fought back, petitioning the court to discharge the receivers and asserting that Knight-Campbell was indeed a going concern with great potential. The judge agreed. Campbell was given back the keys, but not before the receivers staged a massive inventory reduction sale. After two years of fighting, Campbell published another advertisement in May 1935 promising that the "Symbol of Good Music," the knight and the camel, would carry on.

It would, but not in the old way. The Feldhauser Building proved an important asset, allowing Knight-Campbell to move entirely into it, vacating the Paris Building. Into that space moved Wells Music, two rivals now side by side, but with Wells stronger, capturing exclusive Steinway rights, leaving Knight-Campbell with Kimball as their best offering. After KOA Radio occupied the other half of the Paris, it was remodeled and renamed the NBC Building, for KOA's national affiliation. Knight-Campbell continued its association with *The Post*; after the paper phased out youth groups, theater-loving "Miss Helen" Bonfils, its primary owner after her father's 1933 death, created the Denver Post Summer Opera, an annual production at the Cheesman Park Pavilion. This was typically light opera or operetta, and Knight-Campbell provided tryout and rehearsal space on its third floor. Knight-Campbell remained at 1617 until 1970, when it moved to Lakewood; Clarence Campbell died the following month. Wells Music remained in the Paris Building until 1963, when it moved next door to 1641 California. The Paris/NBC Building came down two years later, for a surface parking lot. A parking garage occupies the site today.[28]

S.H. KRESS

The elegant S.H. Kress Building on the eastern corner of 16th and Curtis Streets—three stories high, faced with white terra cotta, adorned with Gothic Revival details above third-floor windows, its street floor lined with display windows on both façades—was not yet a half-century old when Colorado National Bank demolished it in 1965, promising a skyscraper on the site. Instead, the bank converted the land, along with adjacent parcels once occupied by the May Company, into a parking lot; a precast concrete parking garage arose here in 1999, obviously lacking the Kress Building's grace and beauty.

Samuel Henry Kress was born near Allentown, Pennsylvania, in 1863, and opened his first shop in 1887. By 1914, when he leased the Hughes Building's ground floor, on the southern corner of 16th and Stout Streets across from local retailers Gano-Downs & Company and A.T. Lewis & Son, his chain of S.H. Kress & Co. 5-10-25 Cent Stores stretched across more than half of America's states. Kress patronized the arts and architecture and wanted his stores to stand out from his competition (chiefly F.W. Woolworth and S.S. Kresge) through superior design. Beginning in 1905, S.H. Kress maintained a large architectural staff that created "a distinctive yet tasteful presence on Main Street America." Each Kress building typically utilized glazed terra cotta, but styles differed, ranging from Gothic Revival to Art Deco. Interiors were efficient, with well-lit departments selling "affordable, durable, and cheerful" merchandise, along with a lunch counter. The formula worked—by 1927, and continuing for two decades, S.H. Kress achieved "the highest per-store sales of any five-and-dime retailer," its stores celebrated as "beacons of prosperity and progress, exemplars of urban art, and sources of municipal pride."

In 1923, Kress decided Denver's trade was significant enough that the city deserved one of its "Class A" stores, and in 1924, it moved into its new home just two blocks down 16th, across from Joslin's department store and convenient to busy Curtis Street, home to most of downtown's theaters.[29] Kress's architects undoubtedly saw those ornate theaters and realized their building could stand out by being less architecturally rambunctious than the Victory, State and Empress. Yet Kress also harmonized with its cross-alley neighbor, the 1906 May Company, also clad in white terra cotta, with Beaux Arts touches. The Denver Kress store thrived for decades but began losing money in the late 1950s, as retail trade began shifting toward suburbia. The company considered moving up 16th to be near the new May-

The S.H. Kress & Company Building with Curtis Street theaters and the Ernest & Cranmer Building at far left, and the May Company at right, 1930. *Denver Public Library, Western History Collection, X-22611.*

D&F department store at Court Place but instead shut down on December 31, 1960. Its demolition was seen as progress. Although Kress was gone nationally after 1981, many cities and towns across America still take pride in their Kress buildings, including Pueblo, Greeley and Grand Junction.

In 1929, Samuel Kress established a foundation and began donating artworks he had collected over the years to museums; the Denver Art Museum received forty-six paintings and four sculptures.[30]

Montaldo's

Ask a woman of a certain age, and of a certain socioeconomic class, what her favorite store was when she was younger, and instead of mentioning The Denver, Neusteters or Gano-Downs, she might just answer Montaldo's. Catering to well-heeled women of taste, Montaldo's operated at 1632 California Street from August 16, 1938 until 1983, and in other locations continued serving Denver women until 1994. Some might have considered the four-story emporium a department store, but it lacked menswear and other department store features—it was, rather, a specialty store. An early advertisement described Montaldo's fashion ethos: "We insist on chic, but never at the sacrifice of quality. We believe that the well-dressed woman delights rather than astonishes. Our emphasis, therefore, is on loveliness, not on novelty." Another advertisement described the store's "aristocratic feeling for quality."

A Montaldo's customer did not feel as though she was patronizing a link in a multistate chain, yet she was. Corning, Iowa–born Lillian Montaldo, who had previously worked as a department store ready-to-wear fashion buyer, founded the company with her sister Nelle and husband Raymond Doop in the Kansas City suburb of Independence, Missouri, in 1920. Over time, in addition to the Denver store, Montaldo's opened locations in North Carolina (Greensboro, Charlotte, Winston-Salem, Raleigh), Virginia (Richmond), Ohio (Cincinnati and Columbus), Missouri (St. Louis) and Oklahoma (Bartlesville). In Colorado, Montaldo's also operated a boutique at the Broadmoor Hotel in Colorado Springs and, later, a second Denver location. Montaldo's was headquartered in New York, on Fifth Avenue, and Lillian lived in suburban Morristown, New Jersey, but she did not open a New York store because she felt that women in America's smaller cities needed what she had to offer more than those in the metropolis. For new locations, "she liked capital cities and college towns," per a profile; Denver offered both.

Montaldo's maintained a very French feeling throughout its history; this was Lillian's favored aesthetic. The four-story California Street store, a preexisting building remodeled for Montaldo's, resembled a Parisian townhouse, with tall windows and a top-floor mansard-roof effect. Inside, each level was divided into salons, furnished with French antiques and mirrors reflecting elegant light fixtures. Soft lighting flattered the customer, and decor elements combined to evoke luxuriant femininity. Lillian's daughter Barbara Shaw, who ran Montaldo's after her mother stepped down in 1973, remembered Lillian's love of crystal chandeliers, "especially Czechoslovakian" ones.

Montaldo's advertisement, 1971. *Author's collection.*

Lillian Montaldo Doop died in 1980, having lived ninety-five years; Nelle passed four years later at ninety-seven. The last Montaldo's to open, the thirteenth in the

Montaldo's display window, dressed for the holidays, circa 1948. *History Colorado, J. Harford Ryan Collection, 98.283.22.*

chain, arrived in 1978 at Marina Square, a luxury shopping center at East Bellevue Avenue and South Ulster Street on Denver's southern border. In 1983, Montaldo's moved its downtown store one block northwest to 1630 Stout Street. Montaldo's closed this in 1990, moving to the new Cherry Creek (mall). By this time, Lillian Montaldo's vision for upscale shops in secondary cities began to suffer from its primary customers "aging out," with younger shoppers not finding Montaldo's compelling. The chain declared bankruptcy in 1991 and closed Marina Square in 1992 and Cherry Creek in 1994 before declaring a second bankruptcy in 1995, followed by liquidation.[31]

Chapter 4

HOSPITALITY LANDMARKS

American House

Built by John W. Smith on the northern corner of 16th and Blake Streets in 1867–68, American House reigned as Denver's finest hostelry for its first half-decade. Three stories high, of red brick with Italianate windows, it initially featured a wrought-iron second-floor balcony wrapping the corner. At the time, the location on 16th (then called "G Street") would have felt removed from the center of town, raucous and bustling F Street (today's 15th), a decided advantage for guests hoping to sleep.

The hotel's moment of glory came in January 1872, when it hosted Grand Duke Alexei, fourth son of Tsar Alexander II. The twenty-two-year-old Romanov arrived in Denver after hunting buffalo in Nebraska accompanied by William F. Cody, General Philip Sheridan, Lieutenant Colonel George Armstrong Custer and Lakota chief Spotted Tail. Local grandees, having formed the Society of Colorado Pioneers, threw the grand duke a glittering ball at American House, the social highlight of the season. In those years, the hotel also served as a residence for single gentlemen, including young William Garrett Fisher, junior partner in the Daniels and Fisher store.

At the turn of the century, with other hotels boasting finer accommodations, its glory days were over, but it was still respectable, with uniformed bellmen, ideally suited to traveling businessmen on a budget. Three decades later, however, American House was decidedly seedy, with the balcony removed, a fire escape marring the front façade and a portion

American House, circa 1872. *History Colorado, 10040054.*

converted into a cigar factory. After being damaged by the flood resulting from the 1933 failure of the Castlewood Canyon dam, it was demolished that year to build a gasoline station. Today, an early 1980s office building, JP Plaza, occupies the site.[32]

The Inter-Ocean Hotel

Cater-corner from American House at 16th and Blake, the Inter-Ocean superseded the earlier hotel as Denver's finest when it opened in 1873—at least in the opinion of *Rocky Mountain News* editor William Byers. Poet Helen Hunt (later Jackson), who stayed at the Inter-Ocean soon after it opened, held a different view, calling it "one of the most depressing places I have ever seen." Her sentiments prevailed. It struggled, and after several changes, it came under the management of Nelson Sargent, a later operator of American House. He ran both properties simultaneously; the Inter-Ocean's rooms were cheaper. Its failure was not for lack of trying by its first proprietor, Howard C. Chapin. A veteran hotelier who later managed the Grand Central at 17th and Lawrence Streets before moving on to Leadville's Clarendon, Chapin leased the Inter-Ocean from its builder, Barney L. Ford. With Denver still shedding its pioneer roughness, Chapin contracted with Abernathy Brothers of Leavenworth, Kansas, for furnishings and carpets but patronized a local merchant, William B. Daniels & Company (later Daniels and Fisher), for silverware and crockery.

The four-story, red brick Italianate building, designed by William Horace J. Nichols, featured a mansard-roofed fourth floor and, like American House, a wraparound balcony on the 16th and Blake corner. The lobby's semicircular front desk had a black walnut key rack behind it; guests could communicate with the desk via the "Speer patent electric annunciator," which connected

The Inter-Ocean Hotel, circa 1880–90. *Denver Public Library, Western History Collection, C-175; photograph by Joseph Collier.*

all rooms and public spaces. Nearby was a reading room with rich Brussels carpets, marbleized iron fireplace mantel, black walnut writing and reading tables and a three-burner bronze chandelier. In the thirty-five-by-fifty-foot dining room, guests sat around eleven round tables, each accommodating eight to ten people; chairs were black walnut with russet leather upholstery. Three twelve-light chandeliers provided illumination. At the back, the *ne plus ultra* (in Byers's words) kitchen boasted the latest appliances. Also on the main floor was a "ladies' ordinary" room, a lounge where women would not be bothered. This had Brussels carpet of a "beautiful dove color" patterned with light brown oak leaves and bordered in scarlet. A grand staircase led to the second floor, with two more public rooms, a lounge and a music parlor. The balance of this floor was filled with rooms, both suites and singles; upper floors were all single rooms. One reason for the hotel's lack of enthusiastic patronage may have been its bathing and lavatory situation: each floor had a "ladies' and gents,'" but individual rooms lacked facilities. Gentlemen descended to the basement to play billiards; also on this floor were a staff dining room, larder and laundry. "Taken altogether," Byers opined, "the Inter-Ocean is better arranged and better furnished than any other hotel in the territory."

Barney Lancelot Ford, circa 1880. *History Colorado, 10031421.*

Hotel builder Barney Lancelot Ford was one of the most notable African Americans in Colorado history, honored with the only stained-glass window in the Colorado House of Representatives chamber. Born into slavery in Stafford Court House, Virginia, on January 22, 1822, he was the son of the plantation owner, which accounted for his blue eyes and reddish-brown hair; his mother, Phoebe, was enslaved. Barney's owner leased him to a steamboat operator, for whom he worked as a porter, sailing the Apalachicola River from Columbus, Georgia, to the Gulf of Mexico. In 1848, when Barney was twenty-six, his owner transferred him to a Mississippi River passenger steamboat. This proved transformational: in disguise, he walked down the ramp to freedom when the boat docked at Quincy, Illinois. In Chicago, he met two people who changed his life: Henry Oscar Wagoner, correspondent for Frederick Douglass's antislavery newspaper the *North Star*; and Julia A. Lyons, the woman he married and lived with for fifty years. Julia's origins are obscure; some sources claim she was born in South Carolina in 1827 or Indiana in 1821, like Ford with one white and one Black parent, yet the 1870 U.S. census lists her race as white and her birthplace as Ireland. She helped him select middle and last names; he chose "Lancelot Ford" after a steam locomotive he admired. He took up barbering and aided Wagoner's antislavery activities, but in 1851, Ford, with his wife (which was unusual), decided to try the California gold camps. A fugitive slave could not safely travel overland, so they sailed the "Nicaragua route" to Central America, planning to cross the isthmus and re-embark on the Pacific side. They never made it that far; tropical fevers laid them low. They decided to stay, operating the United States Hotel at Greytown on the Gulf coast; Ford also sailed the lake for Commodore Cornelius Vanderbilt's steamboat line, precursor to his planned, never-built canal. The Fords lost their livelihood when the U.S. Navy bombarded Greytown in 1854 "protecting" expatriate Americans from town citizens. They returned to Chicago, where Ford and Wagoner operated a livery stable as cover for an Underground Railroad station.

Again attracted by gold, the Fords arrived in Colorado in May 1860, traveling to Breckenridge, where Ford and some associates staked a claim. This ran afoul of a local white supremacist named Dode, who connived with Summit County's sheriff and Ford's own Denver lawyer, whom he had hired to file the claim, to force Ford out. When Ford would not leave, Dode rounded up like-minded thugs to harass him, or worse. Hearing of Dode's plans, Ford and his friends grabbed their gold, fleeing over a hill that was then named "(racial slur) Hill" for over a century (renamed Ford's Hill in 1964). Ford came to Denver and opened a barbershop on Blake Street near F Street, later adding a café. Built of wood, it burned in Denver's great fire of April 1863, costing Ford his investment. He approached Luther Kountze of Kountze Brothers Bank (later Colorado National) for a rebuilding loan. Kountze lent him $6,000 at 25 percent interest. Ford built a two-story masonry building at (today's) 1514 Blake Street, opening the People's Restaurant, shortly one of Denver's finest dining palaces thanks to Ford's hospitality and excellent cooking. He opened a bar upstairs and another barbershop in the basement (this structure, now three stories, is extant). Ford repaid Kountze's loan in three months; his 1864 income of $4,673 was the fourteenth-highest reported in Denver. In April 1865, Ford hosted a "big ball and festival," largely attended by fellow African Americans, "in commemoration of the fall of Richmond and the downfall of human slavery in the south." Around this time, Ford successfully campaigned against Colorado statehood; a proposed constitution would forbid Black men from voting.

Later that year, he sold the business to Swiss immigrant John J. Reithmann for $23,400 but retained ownership of the building, leasing it for $250 per month, and left some of his affairs in the hands of what turned out to be an unscrupulous agent. Before leaving, he bought three lots at Blake and G (later 16th) Streets where he would later erect the Inter-Ocean. After helping establish adult education classes for freed slaves, Ford returned to Chicago, but in 1867, he was forced to journey to Denver to unsnarl his business interests and take back the restaurant. During this period, he hosted a dinner for several illustrious guests, including banker Jerome B. Chaffee, Denver mayor Milton DeLano and Generals Ulysses S. Grant, William Tecumseh Sherman, Frederick Tracy Dent and Frank Hall. After Ford's death, Hall recounted a conversation he had with Ford in about 1885, when Ford related his life story. Hall's account glosses over some of the worst things that Ford endured, focusing instead on his many businesses. Also during this time, Ford, with Henry Wagoner, who had moved to Denver in 1865, founded an elementary school for Black children after Denver's school board prohibited non-whites from attending its school.

The next stop for Ford, Julia and their two children, Sarah (born 1858) and Louis Napoleon (born 1860), was Cheyenne, the "instant city" created by the Union Pacific Railroad (UPRR) in 1867. Ford opened a hotel, Ford House, gaining the same high reputation he enjoyed in Denver. That did not prevent racists from trying to run him out of business. The railroad aligned itself with a different hotel, Railroad House, with a poor reputation. In May 1869, a UPRR train, instead of proceeding to the depot, stopped directly in front of Railroad House, with passengers encouraged to detrain. At the depot, Ford's porters awaited the train to assist guests to Ford House. Railroad agents ordered them off the platform, prepared to call the local police if necessary. The city marshal was more sensible than the railroaders, declaring that he "favored competition" and refused to cooperate. About four-fifths of the passengers checked in at Ford House, knowing it was the better hotel. The next night, Cheyenne's mayor ordered the police to ensure the railroad would not try its dirty tricks again, telling the press that "if the Railroad House wants the public support, let them get it by keeping a better house than the Ford House—if they can." This chapter ended in January 1870 when a fire swept through, destroying Ford House and costing Ford his $30,000 investment.

Ford returned to Denver to repair his fortunes; a November 1870 newspaper notice advertised "FORD'S People's Restaurant, B.L Ford, Propr." In 1871, he successfully petitioned city council for better drainage on Blake Street, and in August 1872, he bought Sargent House, a three-story brick hotel at 18th and Larimer Streets previously owned by the aforementioned Nelson Sargent. Yet he was not all business: that year, he became the first Black man in Colorado selected for a grand jury, and in 1873, he ran unsuccessfully for a territorial legislature seat.

In 1873, he built the Inter-Ocean, selling it in 1874 to Benjamin O. Cutter. In 1875, new management took over, and the hotel sold again in 1876, at auction, for less than Ford had spent building it. By now, he had left Denver again, building a second Inter-Ocean Hotel in Cheyenne but not keeping it long. Still struggling financially, the Fords moved to San Francisco, where he briefly operated a restaurant. He finally solidified his fortunes permanently by moving to Breckenridge again in 1880, opening Ford's Restaurant and Chop House and investing in a mine. In 1882, he built a nice home at 111 East Washington Avenue, today the Barney Ford House Museum. Selling the mine, he and Julia retired to Denver, where she died in 1899, followed on December 22, 1902, by Barney, who left an estate valued at $16,000. After she died, he boarded with Henry Wagoner, then residing at 2143 Arapahoe Street. The Fords are buried at Riverside Cemetery, Block 20. Hall opined that "there was no worthier citizen nor one more highly respected than Barney L. Ford....Every pioneer will testify to this." The Society of Colorado Pioneers, chaired by Amos Steck, paid tribute also, remembering that "his career in life was marked by many vicissitudes; now moving on the waves of high prosperity and then depressed by misfortune, he always bore himself in a manly attitude and with unshaken courage."

Ford lived eight decades, and the Inter-Ocean Hotel stood for ten. After years as a deteriorating flophouse, it was demolished in 1973 for a parking lot; the mixed-use development 16 Market Square, completed in 2000, occupies the site today. Would a historic building associated with such an important figure be preserved were it threatened with demolition today? We will never know.[33]

The Shirley-Savoy Hotel

Sometimes landmarks are not special for their architecture but for how people use them. The Shirley-Savoy, designed by Willis Adams Marean and Albert Julius Norton, was reasonably handsome, but with the spectacular Brown Palace Hotel located diagonally across 17th Avenue and Broadway intersection, the Shirley-Savoy always seemed more like the sidekick, never

Doc Bird caricature of Shirley-Savoy architect Willis Adams Marean, 1909. *Author's collection.*

the star. Yet it played important roles in Denverites' lives from its opening in 1903 until its 1970 demise. It began as three separate, adjoining hotels: the Shirley on 17th and Lincoln Street, the Savoy at 17th and Broadway and the Shirley Annex on Broadway abutting the Savoy. From the start, however, conjoining them was inevitable. The same architects designed all three, ensuring that floors met once bricked-in arches between buildings were opened, and the Shirley connected to its annex and the Savoy with alley-spanning bridges. Although each portion was built individually, all were of the same buff-colored brick, with similar neoclassical detailing and identical cornice heights. Each had its own personality; had Marean and Norton made them identical, the overall effect would have been monotonous. As designed, the three beautifully complemented each other.

In early years, the Savoy's elegant dining rooms with large windows fronting Broadway attracted well-heeled locals, as *Rocky Mountain News* columnist Pasquale Marranzino remembered: "The public could look in on the diners seated at tables covered with immaculate white napery with a fresh flower centerpiece and a bottle of Manitou Spring Water. In the evening a string quartet did chamber music, and the after-dinner crowd that poured out of the Broadway Theatre up the street kept the place humming." In the 1920s, the Shirley-Savoy attracted crowds to the Rainbow Lane nightclub, young couples gliding to the Joe Mann Orchestra (even as Mann, as an African American, could not rent a guestroom). Proximity to the capitol and reasonable rates attracted legislators from Colorado's hinterland during the legislative session; they nicknamed it "the Bunkhouse." Here they socialized with each other, regardless of party, discussing business over dinner or drinks in the bar, per one account. Marranzino more cynically remembered, "The hotel became the place where most of the state's public business was conducted in a very un-public manner. Smoke-filled rooms, king-making, political assassination, etc." The hotel also was packed every January during the National Western Stock Show. Civic and social groups held luncheons, lodge meetings,

The Shirley Hotel (*left*), the Savoy Hotel (*center*) and the Shirley Annex (*right*), circa 1910. *Denver Public Library, Western History Collection, MCC-291; photograph by Louis Charles McClure.*

senior proms and myriad other events in the hotel's dining and meeting rooms. Coloradans also knew the Shirley-Savoy, even if they never entered its doors, as the longtime home of radio station KLZ.

Colonel David Child Dodge built the Shirley and Shirley Annex, naming them for his hometown of Shirley, Massachusetts. Born in 1837, Dodge, a railroad engineer, built lines in Wisconsin and Illinois before the Civil War (he was not closely related to his contemporary, Union Pacific builder General Grenville M. Dodge). During the war, he served the Union at Chattanooga and Memphis. Afterward, he went back to railroads, arriving to Denver in 1865 as agent of the Chicago and Northwestern. He then worked for the Kansas Pacific, Denver's connection to the East, before joining General William Jackson Palmer's Denver and Rio Grande, becoming general manager in 1880. In 1901, after selling his railroad interest, he diversified, investing in Charles Boettcher's Great Western Sugar Company and the Denver Union Water Company; with extra funds, he decided to capitalize on Denver's growing tourist trade by building a hotel.

To run the Shirley, Dodge recruited one of Denver's savviest hoteliers, Edwin R. Cooper. Less well remembered than his contemporaries Maxcy Tabor and William Bush, Cooper was highly regarded, successfully managing the Hotel Metropole across Broadway from The Brown and managing The Brown itself briefly in 1897. After opening the Shirley, James Boon Lankershim hired him to run his eponymous Los Angeles hotel, with Cooper shuttling between Denver and California. In 1906, he partnered with Frederick Bonfils and Charles Boettcher, buying property at 17th and Champa Streets, where Boettcher erected the Ideal Building. That same year, Cooper joined with Boettcher and Frederick Bailey in the Municipal Traction Company, which unsuccessfully proposed breaking Denver Tramway Company's streetcar monopoly.

As the as-yet-unnamed hotels arose on 17th Avenue in 1902, Dodge decided his was too small. He owned two lots on Lincoln Street, insufficient for what he needed, so when four lots on Broadway, abutting the future Savoy, became available, he snapped them up and hired Marean and Norton to design the Annex. He did not use it entirely for hotel rooms. Denver Union Water Company occupied the ground floor, with the second as rentable offices; the top four floors housed hotel rooms. Combined, the Shirley and Shirley Annex boasted 236 rooms, making it Denver's second-largest hostelry. Cooper bought from local merchants and manufacturers whenever possible. Cooper & Powell Furniture Company (no relation) appointed rooms, with Cordes & Feldhauser providing carpets and draperies. Stearns-Rogers designed and manufactured the boilers, which also powered electric lighting. The Shirley opened in October 1903, with the annex following in spring 1904.

Wealthy Walter Scott Cheesman built the 125-room Savoy. In 1902, prior to deciding to build at 17th and Broadway, he collaborated with Cooper on a proposed hotel for land he owned on Colfax Avenue between Broadway and Lincoln Street, commissioning Frederick J. Sterner for a five-story, neoclassical, U-shaped hotel fronting Colfax that would have complemented the future Civic Center; this did not come to fruition. To furnish the 17th Avenue hotel, Cheesman contracted with Daniels and Fisher to provide "everything from roof to basement," giving the store's E.J. Lindquist, head of its furniture department, "carte blanche to equip the house in a manner to make it the most magnificent hotel between the Mississippi and the Pacific coast." The hotel commissioned western artist Carl Lotave to paint six works, including four murals and two framed pieces for the bar, later the Indian Grill. To manage the hotel, likely named for the London Savoy, Cheesman signed brothers-in-law Charles E. Owen of Colorado Springs and

Postcard showing the Savoy dining room, circa 1905. *Author's collection.*

Denver's Schuyler H. Alexander. The Savoy opened on April 10, 1905, with a luncheon for the Denver Real Estate Exchange. The corner restaurant on Broadway featured floral-design stained-glass transom windows above plate glass and tile floors. Diners enjoyed music provided by Raffaelo Cavallo's orchestra. Upstairs, all rooms had private baths and telephone service. Overall, the Shirley, Annex and Savoy represented an investment of over $900,000 by Dodge, Cheesman and the hoteliers.

Cheesman died in 1907 and Dodge in 1918, their hotels still competing, but by all accounts, the two men remained friendly (Cheesman owned a large stake in the water company). The death that captured the press's attention more than either of these men, however, occurred on May 6, 1914, when hotel guest Colonel James C. Bulger shot and fatally wounded Lloyd F. Nicodemus, a proprietor who had taken over in 1912. Bulger, a Spanish-American War veteran described as a "soldier of fortune" who was recruiting men to fight against Mexico "in case Uncle Sam had to issue a call to arms to adjust the Mexican situation," was blind drunk and had previously come to blows with another guest, Hugh Clark, in the bar, emerging cut and bruised. After Nicodemus's partner Royal K. Starkweather ordered Bulger to leave, Bulger bought two pistols at Tritch Hardware Company and returned, intending revenge on Clark. (Coincidentally, Starkweather had been present three years earlier at an infamous Brown Palace murder.) Bulger staggered through the lobby, pistols in each hand, searching for Clark and threatening guests, including two legislators. Reaching the front desk, he demanded Clark's whereabouts. When Nicodemus replied that he had no idea where Clark was and was going to telephone police, Bulger followed him into the office and shot him. Five female employees were present, having fled the lobby; hotel porter John Quinn tackled Bulger and wrested the guns away.

On his attorneys' advice, Bulger pleaded temporary insanity. He had served in the war's Philippine theater, where he had been wounded by a bullet in the head (self-inflicted) and had been addled by tropical sun; his inebriation further deprived him of judgment. That Colorado was then debating Prohibition played into the case, with the prosecution blaming drink entirely for his mental state, not insanity. Prosecution described how he managed to direct a taxicab to take him to several spots—the hardware store; the Ernest and Cranmer Building, where he consulted with his attorney; and other places prior to returning to the Savoy. He loaded his guns while riding in the cab; clearly, he intended violence. Bulger rebelled, unwilling to be labeled "insane," even if "temporary." The jury deliberated for less than an hour, handing prosecutors the victory and sentencing Bulger to death. His attorneys appealed to the Colorado Supreme Court, which affirmed the lower court's decision. His execution was scheduled and postponed several times, with additional eleventh-hour examinations and sanity hearings. The Woman's Christian Temperance Union weighed in, blaming his drunkenness on a "system which permitted the sale of the liquor"; prominent Progressive Ellis Meredith argued against the death penalty. In late 1916, Governor George Carlson commuted his sentence to life in the penitentiary's insane ward. Shortly after the shooting, city council passed an emergency bill outlawing gun sales to any intoxicated person. In a final irony, in early 1916, once Colorado enacted Prohibition, proprietors of tiny Bulger City, a burg near Wellington in northern Colorado the killer had founded in better days, disassembled its buildings and moved them across the line into Wyoming, where they could still sell alcohol—at least until the Volstead Act.

Even before it opened, rumors proliferated that the hotels would combine; Dodge and Cheesman held negotiations but never quite merged. Finally, in 1921 the Cheesman estate agreed to sell the Savoy for $500,000 to the Shirley, now headed by Dodge's sons John and David C. Jr., creating the Shirley-Savoy, a 375-room behemoth. In 1924, the hotel announced plans to add four guestroom floors to the Annex, with a glassed-in roof garden atop the Savoy. Nothing came of this; instead, in 1925, the hotel inked a deal that ensured years of free publicity as home to Denver's first commercial broadcaster, KLZ Radio, which owner William D. "Doc" Reynolds founded as an amateur station, 9ZAF, in 1920, obtaining its commercial license and call letters in 1922. KLZ built studios on the Shirley's ground floor, erected its one-hundred-foot transmitter on the roof and began broadcasting Joe Mann's Orchestra's dance music into Colorado homes. The hotel erected large neon signs on the roof and down the Savoy's corner, proclaiming "HOTEL SHIRLEY SAVOY" to travelers, visible from Union Station at the lower end of 17th Street; below that, a lightning bolt bisected "KLZ." In 1937, the hotel commissioned George Meredith Musick to design an addition adjacent to KLZ's studios housing the Lincoln Room, a large, high-ceilinged multipurpose auditorium for conventions and concerts broadcast on KLZ; jazz pianist Earl "Fatha" Hines brought his band to it in 1940. KLZ left the Shirley-Savoy in 1954 for new quarters on Speer Boulevard.

View from 17th and Tremont Streets at night, showing the Shirley-Savoy and KLZ neon signage, 1936. *Denver Public Library, Western History Collection, Rh-204; photograph by Harry Mellon Rhoads.*

The Shirley-Savoy thrived through World War II and the early postwar period, but as years passed, visitors favored newer hotels, particularly after 1960, when William Zeckendorf opened the Denver Hilton on nearby Court Place. The hotel seemed old-fashioned; owners tried to overcome that perception through modernization, replacing windows along 17th Avenue and Broadway with solid concrete aggregate walls. Below the cornice, the *Rocky Mountain News* installed a running headline sign wrapping the corner with journalistic excitement, but it attracted no new business. Lacking parking, in 1963 the hotel demolished the Shirley, Shirley Annex and Lincoln Room to create lots, reducing the room count to just the Savoy's 125. In 1968, Columbia Savings and Loan announced a fifty-story tower for the site, but plans were shelved. The hotel closed anyway at the end of January 1970, and in February, wrecking crews came, creating yet another parking lot. The skyscraper plan was revived in 1977; the thirty-six-story, aluminum-and-glass Amoco Tower opened its doors in 1980, with Columbia Savings on the ground floor.[34]

The Windsor Hotel

By the time Sal Paradise, Jack Kerouac's fictional *On the Road* alter ego, hit the Windsor bar in 1950 with Dean Moriarty (Neal Cassady) and a large party, sitting around writing "crazy things" on penny postcards to mail to Carlo Marx (Allen Ginsberg) in New York, surrounded by "fifty glasses of beer," what had once been Denver's finest hotel and high-society hub had less than a decade of life left. Its Larimer Street environs were no longer the center of town, and its neighbors were pawnshops, low taverns and other fleabag hotels.

This was not the original vision. In 1878, Scotsman James Duff arrived in Denver as an agent of a British investment group led by Lord James Barclay. Coming to Colorado to build the High Line Canal, Duff was frustrated by the lack of decent accommodations and convinced his patrons to fund a hotel that would cater to families seeking a quiet environment at affordable prices. Accordingly, the Denver Mansions Company incorporated in London in 1879. However, it was the involvement of Colorado's most flamboyant mining millionaire, Horace Tabor, that transformed Duff's modest notion into the Windsor. A partnership including Tabor, hotelier William Bush and Tabor's Leadville friend Charles Hall made a deal with Duff to operate the hotel. Bush had previously managed Leadville's

The Windsor Hotel, with the Barclay Block at left, circa 1890. *Author's collection.*

Clarendon (owned by Tabor) and Central City's Teller House. Chicago architect William Warren Boyington had completed Montreal's Windsor Hotel in 1878 and was engaged to build a scaled-down Denver version. The palatial hotel at the northern corner of 18th and Larimer Streets opened its doors on June 23, 1880.

Though a mere twelve years separated the opening of American House from the Windsor, Denver had become a completely different town. Fueled by mining riches and now accessible via rail, it required a fine hotel. Tabor and company spared no expense on the five-story, 225-foot-long project, paying $100,000 for land, $350,000 for construction and another $175,000 for furnishings. Exterior masonry—gray rhyolite trimmed in red sandstone—came from Colorado quarries, but nearly everything else derived from Chicago or abroad, including carved black walnut furniture, diamond dust mirrors, Haviland china and seven miles of yard-wide Brussels Axminster carpeting. Gentlemen entered from Larimer and ladies from 18th Street, converging on a marble-floored lobby with a twenty-foot ceiling. The main floor hosted several retail spaces that opened to both lobby and street, along with a barbershop, billiards and two bars, one with a floor embedded with three thousand silver dollars. On the second floor were three dining rooms, reception rooms and a ballroom, its striped German and white maple floor mounted on steel coils (some accounts say cables) for "extra bounce."

The second floor also had guestrooms, including the famous corner bridal suite with balcony. Elaborate staircases trimmed in black walnut and three elevators connected the floors. Other modern conveniences included hot and cold running water in every room, annunciators connecting with the front desk and the latest fire protection systems. The staff numbered 120, its female members residing across the alley in the "Little Windsor," connected via tunnel so these respectable young women would not be seen walking on Market Street, Denver's red-light district. Stories of other tunnels, including one running to Union Station via the Windsor Stables at 18th and Blake Streets, are apocryphal, although the tunnel under 18th Street connecting the Barclay Block was real.

Built by Duff after the Windsor, the Barclay Block contained a series of Roman-style baths in its basement, for Windsor guests and others, with a "Sudsatorium," "Frigidorium," "Lavatorium" and marble swimming pool. The Barclay was the temporary home to the Colorado legislature while the State Capitol was under construction. Members availed themselves of the tunnel for discreet trips to the Windsor's bars without being espied by the press or constituents. When the Windsor opened, a young man recruited from Chicago's Palmer House, Harry Tammen, tended bar. A dozen years later, he and Kansas City lottery operator Frederick Bonfils bought the struggling *Denver Post*. Tammen loved to tell of his time at the Windsor, where he "got [his] first real capital....I used to toss a dollar to the ceiling. If it stuck there, it belonged to the boss. If it fell, it was mine." With the influx of tourists, Tammen developed a more lucrative and honest moneymaking scheme. In 1881, he leased a Windsor retail space for the H.H. Tammen Curio Company, which grew into one of the largest tourist trinket purveyors in the western United States. Later, when Tammen owned the Sells-Floto Circus, he rented Windsor rooms as winter quarters for his performers.

The Windsor's registry held four presidents' signatures: Ulysses Grant, Grover Cleveland, Theodore Roosevelt and William Howard Taft. Literary guests included Mark Twain, Robert Louis Stevenson, Rudyard Kipling, George Bernard Shaw and Oscar Wilde, who was said to be so unhappy with the wallpaper that the hotel changed it for him. To locals, the Windsor's most famous guest was Horace Tabor. His share of the Windsor's operating partnership is unknown but was likely a majority, particularly after his estranged first wife, Augusta, bought Charles Hall's shares. Hearing of this, and not wanting Augusta nosing around, Tabor used Bush as a front to buy those shares from her. Middle-aged Tabor

The Windsor Hotel lobby with black walnut stairway, 1948. *Thomas J. Noel collection.*

was then courting twenty-eight-year-old Elizabeth McCourt Doe and was angling to represent Colorado in the U.S. Senate, with the Windsor as campaign headquarters. Republicans chose Thomas Mead Bowen instead, but Tabor was appointed for a one-month period to finish Henry Teller's term. During that Washington month, Tabor married "Baby" Doe in a Willard Hotel ceremony attended by President Chester Arthur,

The Windsor Hotel bar, as Jack Kerouac would have known it, 1948. *Thomas J. Noel collection.*

Notable Coloradans, including Horace Tabor and Senator Edward Wolcott, imbibe in a Herndon Davis mural, alongside live drinkers in the Windsor Hotel bar, 1948. *Thomas J. Noel collection.*

The Windsor Hotel in its skid row era, circa 1940. *Thomas J. Noel collection.*

but not Mrs. Arthur. Society was scandalized by Tabor's abandonment of long-suffering Augusta and marriage to voluptuous Baby Doe, but Tabor didn't blink, installing his bride in the Windsor's bridal suite and (purportedly) having its doorknobs and bathtub plated in gold. Tabor lost his fortune through bad investments, completely undone by the Panic of 1893; the Windsor changed hands, and Tabor spent years trying to regrow his fortune. By 1899, Tabor's Denver friends had managed to have him appointed as postmaster, and he, Baby Doe and their two daughters moved into room 305, with a Rockies view. It was here, on April 10, 1899, that Tabor died from peritonitis resulting from untreated appendicitis.

When Henry Cordes Brown built his eponymous hotel uptown at 17th and Broadway, he recruited Bush as manager; Bush had previously left the Windsor to open the Hotel Metropole on Broadway. The Brown's 1892 opening marked the death knell for the Windsor, although the glorious invalid would take nearly seven decades to die. By the early 1900s, new operators marketed it to tourists seeking bargain lodgings; things went downhill from there. In 1922, sixty police officers raided the Windsor, shutting down illegal gambling and bootlegging; the district attorney nearly closed the hotel as a menace. In the 1930s, the rear stairway became infamous for a series of suicides. New owners, aware of the hotel's fabled past, hired artist Herndon Davis to paint a mural of famous denizens (salvaged from the Windsor, it now graces the Oxford Hotel's Sage Room). The 1940s saw tours conducted by Horace Tabor's granddaughter Persis Augusta Tabor and appearances by Mae West and a melodrama troupe, the Windsor Players. In 1956, a Kansas City company bought the Windsor, intending to restore it for the 1958–59 Pikes Peak Gold Rush centennial, but plans fell apart. The Windsor closed in 1958, ironically the same year its Montreal namesake burned down. Its fixtures were auctioned (for criminally low prices) in 1959, and in 1960, it was demolished for a parking lot. The Windsor name graces a condominium tower across 18th Street, and in the 1960s, the former Windsor Farm several miles southeast of downtown became Windsor Gardens, a retirement community bordered by the High Line Canal.[35]

Chapter 5

INSTITUTIONAL LANDMARKS

Agnes Memorial Sanitarium

When steel magnate Lawrence Cowle Phipps relocated from Pittsburgh to Denver in 1901 (see chapter 1), he embarked on a philanthropic project to provide a public good, demonstrate his intention to become an important Colorado citizen and prove that he was not a heartless plutocrat. He bought a quarter section, 160 acres, at East 6th Avenue and (modern-day) Quebec Street, midway between the "health suburb" of Montclair and Fairmount Cemetery, setting aside 40 acres for Agnes Memorial Sanitarium. Why he called it that, instead of Agnes McCall Phipps Memorial Sanitarium, is a mystery. We know it memorialized his Scottish mother, who had died of tuberculosis despite the family's wealth and access to top medical care. The site, on high ground, boasted remarkable views of the Rockies, good breezes and plenty of sunshine—thought ideal, as it had been in Montclair founder Baron Walter von Richthofen's time, for helping tuberculosis patients recover from their malady.

Grocery wholesaler Chester S. Morey headed the board of trustees, which included several wealthy citizens: John G. McMurtry, John Campion, Walter Scott Cheesman, Tyson S. Dines, John H. Sawyer and Charles J. Hughes Jr. The trustees' building committee (Morey, McMurtry and Campion) selected Denver's Aaron Gove and Thomas Walsh as sanitarium architects. They had worked with Morey previously on his 16th and Wynkoop warehouse and would later design the central portion of Union Station. They chose the Spanish Colonial style for the sanitarium's

The Agnes Memorial Sanitarium administration building, circa 1911. *Denver Public Library, Western History Collection, X-28650.*

five buildings, which would be built of brick covered in Portland cement, with red tile roofs and cupolas and towers creating a lively composition. Phipps established a five-person medical board headed by Dr. Arnold Stedman and including Dr. George W. Holden. Phipps provided the latter a generous stipend to travel to Europe to study leading tuberculosis sanitaria there and purchase medical equipment.

Agnes Memorial Sanitarium, costing approximately $300,000, entirely funded by Phipps, was complete by summer 1904, and on July 2, the dedication ceremony's audience composed a who's who of Denver's upper crust. Among the guests was Reverend Frederick W. Oakes, proprietor of his own sanitarium on the other side of town (see elsewhere in this chapter). After University of Denver chancellor Henry W. Buchtel prayed, trustee Hughes pronounced, "Here we have built for us a great sanitarium which in its great purpose is not unlike that of the battleship. It has been erected for the purpose of defending the people from that much greater peril than any from which the battleship may deliver us, the great white plague. This disease is one of the barnacles of civilization." Applause for Phipps lasted ten minutes, which must have gratified him, as this was the summer of his divorce.

Aerial view of the Agnes Memorial Sanitarium and farmland that would eventually become Lowry Air Force Base, circa 1920. *Denver Public Library, Western History Collection, Rh-1205; photograph by Harry Mellon Rhoads.*

The sanitarium presented an 860-foot-long façade. Instead of aligning it along a north–south axis to match the street, the architects angled it facing west-southwest to capture afternoon sun. A three-story central administration building housed offices, staff quarters, dining room and well-stocked library with oak bookcases, elegant Persian rugs and "walls of Pompeiian red." On the third floor, patients attended lectures and concerts in an assembly hall furnished with a grand piano. Climbing to it was made easier by the stairs' low six-and-one-half-inch rise. The kitchen was equipped with a sterilizing "dish-washing machine, operated by an electric motor," surely one of Denver's earliest. Adjoining the administration building, connected by open-air cloisters and underground tunnels, were two two-story wings, divided by sex. Each contained forty bedrooms with large windows and transoms above entry doors for free air circulation. Verandas 9 feet deep surrounded both wings on all sides, allowing patients as much outdoor exposure as possible, day and night, when beds could be brought out and privatized with canvas partitions. Despite these deep verandas, rooms were well lit, as Gove and Walsh carefully offset windows so that sunlight entered to the maximum extent possible. Connected

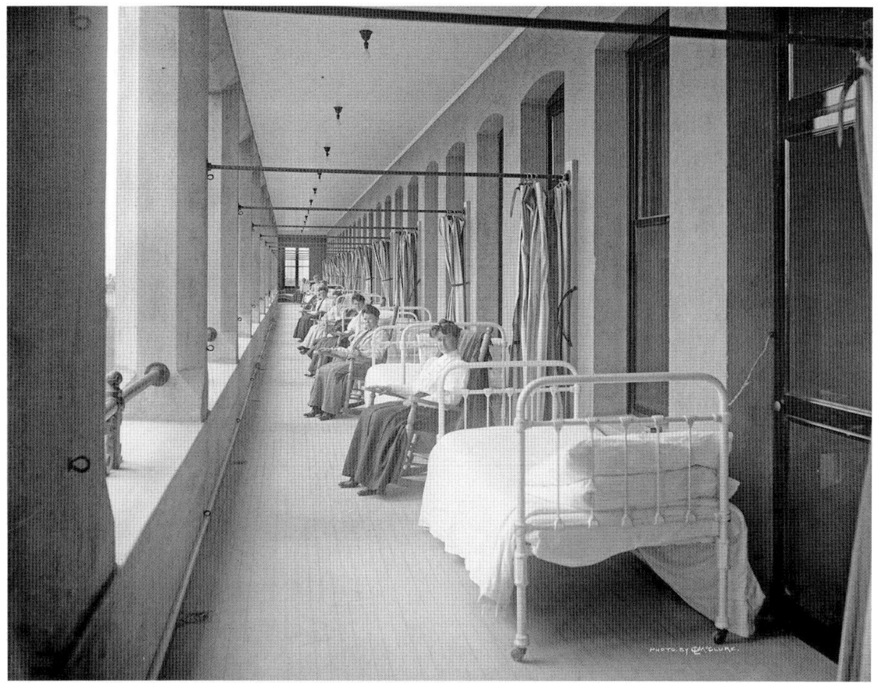

Female residents of the Agnes Memorial Sanitarium on the veranda, circa 1910. *Denver Public Library, Western History Collection, MCC-3554; photograph by Louis Charles McClure.*

to the northern wing, a medical building featured consulting rooms with the most up-to-date equipment, including an elaborate X-ray laboratory and surgical suite. Behind the complex, the fifth building, in the same Spanish Colonial motif and set back 300 feet to keep smoke away from patients, housed a power plant with a towering chimney and the laundry.

The sanitarium was fully occupied shortly after opening, with hundreds on a waiting list. Its patients were not dire cases fated for early death; to be admitted, patients had to provide certificates signed by physicians attesting to their likely recovery. After six months, should a patient remain resident, he or she would be encouraged to depart. Phipps considered funding additional wings but settled on freestanding tents instead, common to other sanitaria. Patients, largely middle class, "the useful members of society" to Phipps, paid $8.50 per week, which was not enough to cover costs, so later it was raised. Phipps established a $300,000 endowment for operating shortfalls. Not every neighbor relished having a tuberculosis sanitarium nearby; Montclair residents suggested it be called the "Agnes Climatic Hotel" to make it seem less threatening.

A patient's bedroom at Agnes Memorial Sanitarium, circa 1920. *Denver Public Library, Western History Collection, X-28655.*

Agnes Sanitarium closed in 1932 after tuberculosis treatment shifted from sanitaria to other regimens. The building would not remain dark for long. In 1934, the U.S. Army Air Corps (predecessor to the U.S. Air Force) looked to relocate its aerial photographic training center from Chanute Field near Rantoul, Illinois. The military required a site with clear skies not prone to frequent cloudiness, and it wanted a nearby bombing range for pilot practice. With political and business leaders promoting it as a huge economic development opportunity, in 1935, Denver voters approved bonds to buy the sanitarium and adjoining land to donate to the Air Corps. The service chose Denver after evaluating eighty-five other sites; that it would come free of charge aided the Air Corps' decision-making. In 1937, the Denver Branch, Air Corps Technical School, opened its doors, with classrooms occupying former examination rooms, laboratories and even attics. In 1938, the facility was renamed for Lieutenant Francis B. Lowry, the only Colorado pilot killed during the Great War. What later became Lowry Air Force Base served many purposes before its 1994 closing, including as logistical base for President

Dwight D. Eisenhower on his many Denver visits. Unfortunately, with a newer, larger base headquarters nearby, "Building 256," as the Air Force numbered the former main sanitarium building, was demolished in 1963.[36]

Arapahoe–Denver County Courthouse

Arguably the single most spectacular act of civic destruction in Denver history (the Skyline Project's demolitions were cumulatively larger), the 1933 razing of the Denver County Courthouse also marked the faint dawning of public awareness that "progress" comes with costs. Just fifty years old, the courthouse came down shortly after its replacement, the City and County Building, opened on Bannock Street. Mayor George Davis Begole, who defeated Benjamin Stapleton's bid for a third term in 1931, offered the building and its block for sale, but in the Depression year of 1932, no buyers came forth. Unwilling to commit tight city funds to maintain it, Begole instead ordered its demolition, which would at least provide temporary employment to some. Begole's fiscal parsimony came at great price to future generations—imagine razing the State Capitol now, a building of similar scale and grandeur, because of maintenance costs. Would not twenty-second-century Coloradans wish they had been alive to see it?

Erecting a courthouse for Arapahoe County, of which Denver was the seat prior to becoming the City and County of Denver in 1902, on the block bounded by Tremont, Wasoola (later Court Place), 15th and 16th Streets, was deeply contentious in the 1870s. The Denver Town Company had deeded the block, a half mile southeast of town, to the Catholic Church in 1860. County courts occupied several rented locations: first at 16th and Larimer Streets (1861–63), then on Larimer between 10th and 11th Streets (1863–73) and finally at 15th and Lawrence Streets. Momentum for a courthouse began building in 1875. County commissioners initially chose a 14th and Larimer site (which later became City Hall), but others proposed the Tremont location, despite its distance from the business district. Still others proposed converting the recently built Arapahoe School on Lawrence between 17th and 18th into a courthouse. In July, Bishop Joseph Machebeuf announced he would sell the block for $18,000. The county came up with $16,000, citizens provided $2,000 and a courthouse would rise once funds were available.

It would be five years before they were, and the fight heated up again in 1880. The *Rocky Mountain News* opined that Tremont was too far for businessmen and lawyers "to travel for the fun of the thing" and pushed a

Lawrence or Arapahoe site, somewhere between 16th and 20th. Arapahoe School again came up, the school board voting to sell to the county, but property owners in developing neighborhoods farther south and east pushed for the already-purchased land. In a letter to the *News*'s editor, anonymous "Pluck" decried moves to abandon the Tremont site as being influenced by the "London company [*sic*] of money lenders and other owners of property in the vicinity of the Windsor [Hotel]." County commissioners were unswayed and issued a request for proposals. On March 31, 1880, they chose a plan by Detroit architect Elijah E. Myers, who later designed the State Capitol. His three-story courthouse, costing approximately $150,000, measured 215 feet wide by 90 deep, and atop its dome, 176 feet above the street, a statue, *Justicia*, proclaimed the building's purpose. In June, following a parade from 15th and Holladay (Market) Streets, the Colorado Grand Lodge of Free and Accepted Masons laid the cornerstone, accompanied by elaborate ceremonies, rites and rituals.

Three years later, citizens celebrated the courthouse's completion in another lavish ceremony attended by throngs of the proud and curious. The total cost was more than double the initial estimate—$302,204.49 by one accounting or $311,602.74 by another—but Denver was booming, and complaints about money expended were rare. Grand, two-story-high courtrooms illuminated by chandeliers had murals by Andrew Killen, "Denver's leading artist at the time" (more of a decorator than fine artist), illustrating Colorado's white pioneer history. On the Tremont side, landscaped grounds featured two elaborate cast-iron fountains, the "first examples of municipal art which Denver had seen," purchased at an eastern foundry. An apocryphal tale tells that the county hired an artist to paint the iron any color he chose, and he opted for "flesh." This aroused the Woman's Christian Temperance Union, and the fountains quickly received a coat of plain silver. Denver's population having grown tremendously over a decade, in 1892, the commissioners spent another $105,000 to build a fourth floor, also modifying the cupola and dome.

Judge Benjamin Barr Lindsey was undoubtedly the courthouse's best-known magistrate, and not just among Denverites—cities in other states and countries modeled their juvenile justice systems after Lindsey's Denver efforts. Born in Tennessee in 1869, Lindsey came to Denver in 1879, eventually enrolling in East High School. After his father's suicide, eighteen-year-old Benjamin became his family's primary financial support. Working odd jobs, he clerked for an attorney, learned the law and passed the bar in 1894. As a protégé of Judge Robert W. Steele, when Steele ascended to the

The Arapahoe County Courthouse from 15th and Tremont Streets, circa 1895. *Author's collection.*

Colorado Supreme Court, he pushed for Lindsey to replace him, and the thirty-one-year-old got the post. His "eureka!" moment came when judging the case of an Italian American boy charged with stealing coal. Learning of the boy's family's hardship, he realized that many juveniles passing through courtrooms and reform schools were merely victims of grinding poverty and began advocating for treating them separately from adult criminals, intervening in home lives if necessary to set them on better paths. Concerned about hygiene, he established showers for them in the courthouse basement until further efforts resulted in construction of the 20th Street Gymnasium and Bath House (extant today). Denver rapidly warmed to Lindsey, and he began attracting national attention. He helped legislators write laws in 1903 that set up juvenile courts statewide.

However, the sometimes-prickly Progressive jurist had objectives beyond juvenile justice and ran afoul of Denver's power brokers. Although he and Mayor Robert Speer were ostensibly of the same (Democratic) party, Speer's close ties not only with business barons—William Gray

Judge Benjamin Barr Lindsey at his desk with juveniles facing him, circa 1910. *Library of Congress.*

Evans, David Moffat and others—but also with Denver's less savory elements, including gambling kingpin Ed Chase and the Market Street madams, offended Lindsey's moral sense. In 1908, with journalist Ellis Meredith, Lindsey published *The Rule of Plutocracy in Colorado: A Retrospect and a Warning*, but it was his next project, which muckraking journalist Upton Sinclair claimed credit for inspiring, that really alienated Denver's oligarchs. Serialized in the national *Everybody's Magazine*, "The Beast and the Jungle," polished by writer Harvey J. O'Higgins, appeared beginning in September 1909. It recounted Lindsey's battles with "Napoleon" Evans, "Boss" Speer and others on behalf of ordinary people. He described the view from his chambers, where "I can see the Majestic Building from which the corporations govern the state. What a government! And what an opposition! The millionaire uses the power of his wealth to rob and starve and pollute a whole community with protected vice and thwarted justice and laws defied." Frederick Bonfils's *Denver Post*, then battling reformist Thomas Patterson's *Rocky Mountain News*, lambasted Lindsey as a "withered soul" but still published excerpts. In 1910, the installments appeared in book form as *The Beast*, earning praise from Theodore Roosevelt and others.

After World War I, America turned more conservative, and muckraking lost favor. Ever the crusader, Lindsey butted heads with the Ku Klux Klan. In 1924, this terrorist group managed to capture the Colorado governorship (Clarence Morley) and Denver mayoralty (Stapleton), and Lindsey spoke out, labeling its members "sadistic savages." In revenge, Klan-allied politicians and judges engineered his downfall, removing him in 1927 from his judgeship. Lindsey burned the juvenile court's records to prevent the Klan from obtaining them, and after his Colorado disbarment on an unrelated matter, he moved to California, where he died in 1943. His widow, Henrietta, received personal condolences from President Franklin Roosevelt. In 2009, the city, having long celebrated less worthy names, honored Lindsey's memory by co-naming its new judicial center the Lindsey-Flanigan Courthouse for him and James Flanigan, the first Black Denver district court judge.

The courthouse would not long outlast Lindsey's Denver career. At its dedication, the *Denver Republican* declared it would "remain an ornament to the city and county so long as it shall stand," those final six words foreshadowing that one day it would not. In 1901, historian Jerome Smiley considered it "not such an edifice as would now be built for public purposes, [but] it is a handsome, commodious and well-arranged building," and pointed out that its site, controversial decades earlier, "was a most fortunate selection....The property probably could now be sold for upward of a half million dollars." Indeed, in 1912, Milton D. Guldman, son of Golden Eagle department store founder Leopold Guldman, proposed paying Denver $900,000 for the site once the city built its expected new courthouse facing Civic Center. He and his father envisioned a new twelve-story building housing their relocated store along with a fine hotel.

Pressure for a new courthouse mounted in the 1920s, as the old building grew increasingly crowded. Voters authorized buying land across Bannock Street from Civic Center in 1923 and approved construction bonds in 1925. As with all municipal projects, opposition formed, led by *The Denver Post*, no Stapleton fan. In 1928, it opined, "If Denver must have an old-fashioned courthouse, why not refurbish the present structure and save for the taxpayers the 2 million-odd dollars the Stapleton administration proposes to spend for the old-fashioned municipal building [planned] for the Bannock Street site," disparaging its design as something "which might

Intersection of 16th and Tremont Streets as seen from the Denver County Courthouse dome, circa 1908. Only one building in this photograph remains standing. *Author's collection.*

serve excellently for a backwoods community, but is completely out of tune with the trend of the day in enlightened and forward-looking cities." That was classic Frederick Bonfils–ism, but the new building's design, by a consortium of Denver architects, had another, more sophisticated opponent: architect Jules Jacques Benoit Benedict.

In early 1932, Mayor Begole put the block up for sale for "nothing less than one and one-fourth million dollars" and promised, "If the property isn't sold, the courthouse building will be razed and the block will be made into a public park." Benedict did not want the property sold; he foresaw that Denver might need it as it grew. Nor should the building disappear. In an essay for *The Post* he wrote, "We revere the past because of its expression of man's creation. Expression, no matter how grandiose or naive, is impossible for us to duplicate, or yet even imitate, because we have either progressed or retrograded far from the state of mind that created them." Instead of demolishing the courthouse, Benedict, leading a "public-spirited group of citizens," proposed modifying it to house a combination museum and exhibition hall. He would replace the lawns with a one-story addition built to the sidewalk on all sides, with halls displaying "automotive, mining, radio and television equipment," with manufacturers paying for exhibition space. A pioneer museum with covered wagons, log cabins, plows and other artifacts would educate schoolchildren and tourists alike in Colorado's history. "Our building is up and ready for occupancy," he concluded. "Let's don't destroy it."

Yet destroy it they did. Benedict unveiled his proposal in December 1932, but in January 1933, the Denver Real Estate Exchange informed Begole that he would never get his asking price and advised demolition. "The biggest wrecking job ever done in Denver" commenced that fall. In early 1933, *The Post* mourned the denouement of the lady that had crowned the building: "Expelled from her habitation, Justice was loaded upon a truck, driven away, and vanished as if into thin air....What has become of her? HAS JUSTICE VANISHED FOREVER? Now she has vanished, as the building shortly will vanish after her. What will become of Justice?" No one knew, but parts of the building survived, hauled to other places; *The Post* itself ultimately snagged *Justicia*. Killen's murals had been removed in 1903 and given to the Colorado Historical Society. The Masons received the 1880 newspaper-filled cornerstone. Decorative cast-tin griffins went to Central City Opera, which lost or disposed of them, but two iron lampposts, of eight that had framed the four entrance doors, stand today on Central City's Eureka Street flanking the opera house.

City crews built a reflecting pool where the courthouse had stood, and the full-block park (although never formally dedicated as such) renewed spirits of Denverites battered by the Depression and war. In 1943, Henrietta Lindsey scattered her husband's ashes where the judge had once toiled. The land remained for sale, and in 1945, a Stapleton crony, realtor Burr Bret Harding, accepted the mission of finding a buyer. Traveling to New York, he met with developer William Zeckendorf, who sensed a potential goldmine (literally, as it turned out). The full story of Zeckendorf's efforts to build Courthouse Square, anchored by a department store and hotel, reminiscent of the Guldmans' 1912 plans, is told elsewhere (see the author's *Daniels and Fisher: Denver's Best Place to Shop*, chapter 7). Ironically, this block witnessed a second destructive act in 1995–96, when Zeckendorf's creation, the I.M. Pei–designed hyperbolic paraboloid fronting the May-D&F department store and adjacent ice skating rink, was demolished, to the dismay of many, while another mayor concerned with city finances looked on.[37]

CITY HALL

The City and County Building replaced not just the courthouse but also City Hall, a Victorian heap wedged onto a too-small trapezoidal block bounded by Larimer, Market and 14th Streets and Cherry Creek. It was not beloved; in 1901, Jerome Smiley described it as "in many respects a regrettable edifice. As a building it is a fine and substantial one, but it is lamentably destitute of attractive architectural elements. Its location is unfortunately bad, and the configuration of the plot of ground on which it stands was the chief obstacle in the way of making it such a building as the permanent home of Denver's city government should have been." More recent historians concurred, calling it "no thing of beauty. Its poorly proportioned tower, its cluttered mansard roof, and its awkward rear additions made an unsightly pile that would have been a blot on the landscape had there been any landscape to blot." These shortcomings justified its demolition to many, yet 1880s Denverites were proud of it. When its cornerstone was laid on November 13, 1881, a parade led by Denver's Zouave Band and several Masonic lodges preceded a ceremony officiated by Governor Frederick Walker Pitkin and Mayor Richard Sopris. An estimated crowd of five hundred attended—not the last large throng to assemble at 14th and Larimer.

Denver's first city hall was a wooden structure built on stilts over Cherry Creek, the site chosen to show no favor between formerly independent Auraria and Denver City. The flood of 1864 carried it away, and until the permanent City Hall was completed in 1883, Denver's government occupied rented spaces. Architects William Horace J. Nichols and Leo Canmann designed the new edifice. Less well remembered now, Nichols arrived in Denver in 1872 and swiftly became the young city's leading architect, designing the Inter-Ocean Hotel, First National Bank (later called Constitution Hall) and homes for the wealthy; his best-known extant works are Larimer Square's Gallup-Stanbury Building and University of Denver's Evans Chapel. For the City of Denver, Nichols and Canmann—faced with extensive requirements including governmental offices, council chambers, headquarters for both police and fire departments and a jail—were obliged to completely fill the cramped site rather than setting it apart with landscaping. The four-story stone building (three floors plus a mansard-roofed fourth) cost $225,000, including land, although contractor McPhee & McGinnity won by bidding just $153,000, applying frequently for additional funds, thus inaugurating the time-honored tradition of cost overruns on municipal projects that continues today. The architects designed a 24-foot-wide, 115-foot-tall clock

City Hall, circa 1883. *Thomas J. Noel collection.*

tower on the Larimer side and a fire lookout tower with alarm bell on the Holladay (later Market) side above the fire station. The mansard floor had a slate roof and cast-iron windows. Such was the site's awkwardness that while the Larimer Street façade measured 103 feet wide, the Holladay side measured just 40.

McPhee & McGinnity conveyed the building to the city on March 21, 1883, and it served as City Hall until 1932, when municipal government removed to the City and County Building. It continued serving as police headquarters until that department built a modern replacement at 1245 Champa Street in 1941. The fire department continued using it for communications and for Engine Company No. 6. Yet City Hall had not aged well: a 1901 fire destroyed the top floor, which was not replaced. By 1946, the front portion, vacant since 1941, had most of its windows broken out, and pigeons roosted in the clock tower. The fire department proposed tearing down the Larimer-facing portion to make room for new headquarters and advertised for bids. The lowest—$15,000 plus salvage—came from Lester Frederick Smith of Golden (the Market-facing portion was razed later). Smith family lore maintains that it was his idea to save the clock tower's bronze bell to memorialize the lost landmark; he loved building more than destroying but had a family to support (Smith was the author's grandfather). Whether or not family legend is true, the bell has long been mounted on a concrete pedestal at the 14th and Larimer corner, surrounded by a green patch unofficially called "Bell Park."

No discussion of City Hall is complete without recounting one of the oddest episodes in Denver history, the 1894 City Hall War, which pitted Colorado governor Davis Hanson Waite against his own appointees. An attorney originally from Jamestown, New York, Waite had served in the Wisconsin and Kansas legislatures before arriving in Leadville in 1879. In 1880, he relocated to Aspen and built a reputation as a pro-labor newspaper publisher. That Populist (People's Party) Waite was even elected in 1892 was miraculous, so dominant were Republicans and Democrats, but, as happens in troubled times, both were riven into factions, and four candidates vied for the governorship. Neither the "Silver Democrats" nor the "Silver Republicans"—both tied to Colorado's dominant industry—managed to win a plurality, so Waite won. He immediately alienated many with an extralegal scheme to send Colorado silver to Mexico for minting into "Fandango Dollars," meant as legal tender. In July 1893, with the economy freefalling, he acquired the nickname that dogged him when, in

City Hall (Denver Police Department headquarters) viewed from across Cherry Creek, circa 1935. *Denver Public Library, Western History Collection, X-20749.*

City Hall's narrow Market Street façade, with garage doors for Denver Fire Department Engine Company No. 6, circa 1925. *Denver Public Library, Western History Collection, MCC-3740; photograph by Louis Charles McClure.*

a pro-silver, anti–President Grover Cleveland speech at Denver's Coliseum Hall, he proclaimed, "It is better, infinitely better, that blood should flow to the horses' bridles rather than our national liberties be destroyed." Forever after, his enemies jeered at "Bloody Bridles Waite."

Denver was not then a home-rule city, and governors appointed boards overseeing police, fire and other departments. Denver's government was notoriously corrupt, overly friendly to—and often in the pockets of—liquor, gambling and prostitution interests. Even Waite's harshest critics agreed that his morals were essentially pure, that he stood against vice in all forms. In 1893, he appointed Jackson Orr, D.J. Martin and A.J. Rogers to oversee fire and police departments but soon became disillusioned by their apparent indifference to vice; when he learned in January 1894 that Martin and Orr had actually provided police protection to a gambling operation, he demanded their resignations. They refused; two months passed. On March 14, Waite decided that if they would not leave voluntarily, he would force

City Hall War, March 1894. *Thomas J. Noel collection.*

their physical ouster from City Hall. He activated the First Regiment of Colorado Infantry, along with the Chaffee Light Artillery, which arrived with Gatling guns and howitzers. Inside City Hall, more than two hundred police officers and Arapahoe County deputies prepared the building's defense using Winchester rifles and dynamite. Waite, who lived on California Street, did not come down to Larimer to take command and stopped short of ordering the infantry to fire, instead contacting the commander of nearby Fort Logan, who sent in three hundred regular U.S. Army troops. Huge crowds gathered, nearly surrounding City Hall.

Denver's power brokers were horrified, and on March 15, the chamber of commerce deputized a committee to meet with Waite and urge him to stand down; notables in this group included William Byers, Charles Kountze, Donald Fletcher, David Moffat, Finis Ernest, Jacob Appel, John Jay Joslin, Walter Cheesman, Roger W. Woodbury, William Evans, George Tritch and others. Here was, per Smiley, the "extraordinary spectacle of a committee of citizens appointed to appeal to the Governor of the State to refrain him from precipitating civil war in the State's capital city." Smiley credited their efforts with turning the tide. The forces inside and outside City Hall remained, however, as did the crowds, so on Friday, March 16, the committee again met with Waite and convinced him that the Colorado Supreme Court was the appropriate arbiter. The Fort Logan troops were sent home, and calm returned; on March 25, the court ruled that while Waite could legally remove the commissioners, he had no right to use militia to do so. Orr and Martin still refused to leave. Waite threatened to ignore the court, but it finally ordered the two to surrender their offices, and they complied. Gubernatorial terms were then two years, and later in 1894, Waite again faced three others at the polls. This time he lost, badly, thanks partly to the law he had signed enfranchising women. These new voters, not wanting to reward his casual embrace of military force, sent him back to Aspen.[38]

House of the Good Shepherd

Most landmarks are lost to demolition, but some succumb to flame, and that's what happened, spectacularly, to House of the Good Shepherd at 1401 South Colorado Boulevard. In 1883, Colorado bishop Joseph Machebeuf requested nuns from the St. Louis house of the Congregation of Our Lady of Charity of the Good Shepherd to set up a Denver home for girls and young women. The order supported orphans, those whose families had failed them or who had fallen (or were in danger of falling) into prostitution. Their first home occupied two houses on Galapago Street near downtown, and in 1885, they opened a larger facility on South Cherokee Street. During this period, the House accepted girls from North Dakota as part of the Office of Indian Affairs' reeducation of young Native Americans, forcing them to forget their own culture and adopt Euro-American ways. The Sisters were victims of anti-Catholic prejudice in these years, particularly in the mid-1890s, when Governor Albert McIntire and Denver mayor Marion Van Horn forbade public funding for the House, even though it served charges sent there by public courts. By 1900, approximately three hundred girls and young women called the House home.

In 1911, requiring more room and wanting farther distance from the sinful city, the Sisters purchased twenty acres, a four-city-block spread bounded by Colorado Boulevard, South Jackson Street and East Louisiana and Florida Avenues. The Knights of Columbus raised money, and over two thousand people witnessed the cornerstone ceremony, with speeches by Bishop Nicholas Matz and Governor John Shafroth. Three stories high,

The House of the Good Shepherd, 1933. *Denver Public Library, Western History Collection, X-28906; photograph by Rocky Mountain Photo Company.*

Aerial view of the House of the Good Shepherd, 1930; Colorado Boulevard runs from the mid-left to the top center of the photograph. *Denver Public Library, Western History Collection, X-28905.*

the House cost over $200,000 to build and was split into two sections. One housed orphaned and dependent girls under age twelve, with the other for women. It included St. Euphasia School, where residents learned home economics. A beautiful garden and chapel, built later, catered to spiritual needs.

The new House, with a capacity of 650, could not have opened at a better time. In that Progressive era, after reformer Henry Arnold replaced vice-friendly mayor Robert W. Speer in 1912, the city shut down the Market Street brothels. Activist Josephine Roche, newly appointed as inspector of amusements under police commissioner George Creel, steered the unemployed prostitutes toward the House, where they were treated for disease and taught acceptable morals. A 1931 fire caused damage, but quick-acting residents and nuns led by Sister Mary of the Visitation prevented total destruction. Over time, the House's population dwindled as societal needs changed, and by the 1960s, Colorado Boulevard had become southeast Denver's primary commercial strip. The Sisters sold their valuable property in 1968 to F.R. Orr Construction and built a new facility in Aurora. While it was sitting empty awaiting demolition, the building attracted break-ins, and on a cold January night in 1969, another fire broke out, possibly set by neighborhood teens igniting fireworks. Three alarms later, the House of the Good Shepherd was gone. Orr built an office complex in its place.[39]

Oakes Home

Billed as a "home [with] light, airy, cheerful rooms, abundance of sunshine, good food, and general comforts in pleasant surroundings," the Oakes Home for Consumptives constituted the life work of its namesake, Reverend Frederick Warren Oakes. Born in Troy, New Hampshire, in 1860, he always maintained, curiously, that he had been orphaned at eight. Actually, his father died when he was fourteen, and his mother remained living until 1922; why he called himself an orphan is mysterious. After graduating from Lewiston, Maine's Bates College, he studied at Yale, obtaining a divinity degree. Oakes with his wife, Mabel, came to Colorado in 1892, taking a position in a Leadville Congregational church, but after seven months, he moved to Denver and switched his denomination. Bishop John Franklin Spalding of the Colorado Episcopalian Diocese installed him in 1894 as rector of All Saints Church (1890; now Our Merciful

Savior) at West 32nd Avenue and Wyandot Street in North Denver. Oakes, a money-raising genius, paid the church's $10,000 construction debt in six months.

Oakes saw that tuberculosis patients favored Denver and discovered that most sanitaria and hospitals were institutional, not homelike, even though people lived in them for months. A home away from home, he thought, would better help people heal. His project would be strictly for patients who had good chances of recovery, not the incurable. It would not be for the indigent but for "people of culture and refinement, of brains and education," who would need letters from Christian clergymen attesting to good character. It would not be a for-profit business but would charge "moderately well-to-do" guests nominal sums to cover meals: six dollars per week, later increased to forty-five dollars per month. Oakes understood that tuberculosis patients, even somewhat well-off ones, suffered reduced income, and he wanted their "self respect [to remain] untouched." Operating costs would come from willing philanthropists, and Oakes was well connected.

He consulted with Spalding, who approved the plan, and Oakes teamed with local financier David Moffat and tuberculosis expert Dr. Samuel A. Fisk to locate a site, raise money and establish care standards. Oakes did not have to look far: just one-half mile west, across Denver city limits at Gallup Avenue (today's Zuni Street), was a full, undeveloped square block in the Potter Highlands section of the town of Highlands. (Denver annexed Highlands in 1896.) The boundaries were West 32nd and West 33rd Avenues and Decatur and Eliot Streets (modern names). Both 33rd and Decatur were not "cut through," existing only on paper as future thoroughfares. This detail would come to harm relations with some neighbors.

Oakes first looked to wealthy Denverites for funds; he received his first check from Mrs. Frederick J. Bancroft, wife of a prominent physician. It was soon apparent that Oakes's grand plans could not come to fruition with local funds only, so he boarded an eastbound train and returned with ample donations, most of them in five figures. Among the benefactors were Emily Thorn Vanderbilt Sloane, daughter of William Henry Vanderbilt and granddaughter of Cornelius; Ellen Schermerhorn Auchmuty; William Colford Schermerhorn (who paid for fencing the property); Mrs. Isaac Bell; Morris Ketchum Jessup; and "other wealthy New York friends."

By spring 1895, the first sections of the $100,000-plus facility were ready for patients. Architect Frederick J. Sterner designed it in a sedate, New England Colonial mode, utilizing light yellow brick with white trim.

Oakes Home, 1934. *Author's collection.*

The central portion, named Grace House for New York's Grace Episcopal Church, featured a dramatic columned entry. Here were administrative offices, a music room with a grand piano, a two-thousand-volume library, a billiard room, a gymnasium, dining rooms and, upstairs, two-room suites "for mothers and sons or husbands and wives." Furnishings in common rooms evoked home, with comfortable chairs and sofas, potted plants, oriental rugs, paintings and etchings and the standard bric-a-brac that cluttered the era's interiors. Guestrooms featured iron bedsteads trimmed in brass and handsome case pieces. Flanking Grace House on the west, and connected by ground-floor "cloisters" to it, was Emily House, for women. Its eastern twin, St. Andrews House for men, opened in 1896. All bedrooms included bedside buttons to summon a matron should residents feel ill. A fourth building, also connected by cloister, was Heartsease, completed in 1897 for sicker patients requiring more care. In 1903, Oakes dedicated the Chapel of Our Merciful Savior, where he conducted services every Sunday until his retirement. An anonymous New Yorker paid its $30,000 cost. This Sterner-designed chapel, based on Christopher Wren's London churches, is the only portion of the main Oakes Home extant today.

Despite Oakes's pledge that the Home would charge only nominal fees, some people, although not absolutely poor, could not afford it, so in 1902, across (future) 33rd Avenue on the Eliot corner, Oakes opened the Mrs. Charles L. Adams Memorial Home, operated by and connected to via tunnel, but not officially part of, the Oakes Home. Mrs. Adams's widower, a New Yorker, paid its $50,000 construction cost; it later became the Belle Lennox Hall for Boys, operated as a boarding school, and remains standing today as Lennox Guest Home, an assisted living facility. Near it, Oakes opened in 1902 the Abby Sherwood Jessup Memorial Cottage. This home, with seven rooms and two large verandas, was for patients

A dining room in the Oakes Home or one of its satellite buildings, circa 1915. *Denver Public Library, Western History Collection, MCC-3952; photograph by Louis Charles McClure.*

almost well enough to leave the Oakes Home, no longer requiring close medical supervision; Morris Jessup paid for it. Also in this row was the charming Anne Schermerhorn Memorial Workshop, where Oakes Home guests learned arts and crafts; this Tudor Revival house, which remains standing at 2817 West 33rd Avenue, housed the Blue Unicorn Tea Room in the 1930s.

Not everyone viewed the Oakes Home as a neighborhood blessing. In exchange for tunneling under future 33rd Avenue, neighbors petitioned for Oakes to open that street and Decatur between 33rd and 32nd. Oakes considered the latter ground part of the Home's property and refused; it remains unopened today. More threatening than neighbors' petitions was the Home's tax-exempt status. Oakes always portrayed it as charitable, even though it did not officially accept charity cases. In 1903, after several years of Oakes refusing to pay taxes, Judge Frank Johnson ruled that Oakes Home must pay. He declared it was "run on the same principle as a hotel," that its "expensive and luxurious interior decoration" made it the opposite of a charitable institution and that its main customers were "well off Easterners." The Colorado Supreme Court reversed his decision.

The Oakes Home continued serving tuberculosis patients as years passed; by the early 1930s, it had served between seventeen thousand and twenty thousand (estimates vary). Temple Hoyne Buell, later a prominent Denver architect, was one of them. In 1933, the seventy-three-year-old Oakes announced his retirement. The diocese faced a quandary, as no one could replace him. Numbers were declining; changes in medical treatment worked against the Home, and the resident population was far below capacity. On May 1, 1934, the Home closed, the diocese announcing it as temporary. Which it was: on September 2 it reopened, now operated by the (Episcopal) Sisters of St. Anne, its mission expanded beyond tuberculosis to include other chronic diseases, with "charity extended to worthy patients." This lasted until January 1941, when it closed again. This coincided with the golden wedding anniversary of Fredrick and Mabel Oakes, now living in La Jolla, California (after Mabel died, Oakes relocated to Philadelphia to live with a daughter; he died there in 1951).

In 1942, the Denver Housing Authority considered the Oakes Home for housing war workers, but it remained dark. In 1943, the diocese nearly demolished it but held off due to the war-related housing shortage; also that year, United Air Lines considered it for a dormitory for pilot trainees. Instead, the diocese sold the Home for $67,500 to the (Roman Catholic) Little Sisters of the Poor of St. Francis Seraph of Perpetual Adoration, operators of St. Anthony's Hospital. The nuns moved their administrative offices to the former Grace House. The onetime Emily House became a home for Franciscan Sisters, and the St. Andrews House a home for retired nuns. The Little Sisters owned the Oakes Home until 1974, then selling it to Colorado Springs–based Sisters of St. Francis, who envisioned a retirement home. Faced with a nearly eighty-year-old property saddled with decades of deferred maintenance, the Sisters made a decision that was right for them, demolishing the Oakes Home to build a fourteen-story tower, the Gardens at St. Elizabeth, in its place, completed in 1988. Thankfully, the Chapel of Our Merciful Savior, now Christ the King, remains standing, with recent changes to the grounds making it more visually prominent. City council declared it a landmark in 1974.[40]

QUEEN OF HEAVEN ORPHANAGE

Denver was once dotted with orphanages, many operated by Catholic orders. All are gone, their buildings either repurposed or demolished. From an architectural standpoint, one of those lost buildings deserved better than to be replaced by a chain motel: Regina Coeli, the Queen of Heaven. This North Denver landmark at Federal Boulevard and West 48th Avenue, with its four-story crenelated mass and central six-story tower designed by John Huddart, was visible for miles. The institution's founder, Frances Xavier Cabrini, became the first American citizen canonized by the Roman Catholic Church, patron saint of immigrants, hopeless causes and India.

Maria Francesca Cabrini was born in 1850 in the Italian kingdom of Lombardy-Venetia, then part of the Austrian Empire. She took vows in 1877, adopting the name of the patron of missionaries, and in 1880, she founded the Missionary Sisters of the Sacred Heart. Nine years later, seeking Pope Leo XIII's permission to establish missions in China, he urged instead she travel to America, where so many of her fellow Italians had begun new lives: "Not to the East, but to the West," he directed. Although met with resistance from New York's Archbishop Michael Corrigan, she and her Sisters immediately began establishing schools, hospitals and orphanages in New York and elsewhere. In 1902, Colorado's Bishop Nicholas Matz and Father Mariano Lepore, pastor of North Denver's Our Lady of Mount Carmel, an Italian parish, invited Cabrini to Denver. The city's Italian immigrant community was approximately twenty-five years old, its earliest members first residing in "the Bottoms" near the South Platte River before moving up the hill into North Denver. The clergymen, knowing of Cabrini's reputation for institution building, knew she could help them serve Denver's Italians. Cabrini agreed, soon arriving with several Sisters. In June 1902, they founded Mount Carmel School in the home of businessman Michael Notary at 3357 Navajo Street.

Two years later, given charge of two orphaned girls, the Sisters housed them on the Notary home's third floor. With additional girls needing care, Cabrini searched for a permanent home, purchasing an old farmhouse on seven acres at West 48th Avenue and Boulevard F (today's Federal). Villa Regina Coelhi, the Queen of Heaven Orphanage, formally opened in 1905. Contrary to popular imagination, many girls at Queen of Heaven were not entirely bereft of families. In many cases, they came from single-parent households, and needing to work for a living, these parents relied

Queen of Heaven Orphanage, 1946. *Author's collection.*

on the orphanage to care for their children during the workweek, with the girls returning home on weekends. The Sisters conducted a school where girls were taught, per Cabrini's wishes, to revere religion and live virtuously. To help pay their board, nuns taught them embroidery, selling decorated

Classroom in the Queen of Heaven Orphanage, circa 1922. *Denver Public Library, Western History Collection, X-28935; photograph by Rocky Mountain Photo Company.*

towels and tablecloths to Denver matrons. It was not all work, however; they enjoyed plenty of sunshine, playing outdoors. (An orphanage for boys, Mount St. Vincent, operated nearby at 4159 Lowell Boulevard, overseen by the Sisters of Charity.)

In 1910, Cabrini, to provide the girls even more sunshine, founded a summer camp on Lookout Mountain southwest of Golden. She found an old ranch for sale and raised funds to buy it. High above Mount Vernon Canyon, the site apparently was dry, but in 1912, after Sisters complained of long treks to fetch water, Cabrini instructed them to "lift that rock over there and start to dig. You will find water fresh enough to drink and clean enough to wash." It was so; today, the summer camp is the Mother Cabrini Shrine. Cabrini left Denver and died in 1917 in a Chicago hospital she had founded. That year, the Denver Sisters realized that the old farmhouse, even with an addition they had built, was too small for the 160 girls now calling it home. They raised money, hired architect Huddart and in 1921 opened the new building. During construction, the girls and Sisters acted as hod carriers, ferrying bricks and mortar to the workmen.

Orphan life carried on. In 1938, Pope Pius XI beatified Cabrini, and in 1947, Pius XII canonized St. Frances Xavier Cabrini. On February 16, 1962, with the orphanage serving fewer orphans each year, administrator Sister Ignatius Miceli received a call from Stapleton International Airport. A planeload of young Cuban girls had just landed from Fort Lauderdale as part of Operación Pedro Pan. This was a clandestine evacuation of over fourteen thousand minors from Cuba, their parents fearing mass reeducation programs under the Castro regime. Sister Miceli accepted the girls, ages six to eighteen, teaching them English. This was Queen of Heaven's last notable event; in 1964, the Sisters sold off most of the land to the Colorado Department of Transportation to build the Federal Boulevard off- and on-ramps to Interstate 70. In 1967, orphanage operations ceased after a court decreed that orphans would be better served in foster care. The Sisters established a short-lived Mother Cabrini Memorial School, open to all girls, but it closed in 1969. In 1973, the fifty-two-year-old landmark came down.[41]

University of Colorado Medical School Campus

Only one historic structure remains at an erstwhile forty-acre complex that saw the births, illnesses and deaths of untold numbers of Coloradans; provided employment to thousands of doctors, nurses, professors, researchers and staff; and saw a formerly insignificant regional medical school grow into a major institution. Its buildings spanned seven decades, the first completed in 1924 and the last in 1996, the very year when University of Colorado's regents voted to move the campus to Aurora.

The medical school was four decades old when the campus opened, having been founded in 1883 as the Department of Medicine, occupying part of Old Main on CU's Boulder campus. Two years later, the first University Hospital opened in its own building, followed by Medical Hall in 1888. Early years proved difficult; Boulder was small, and medical schools require large nearby populations for students to learn their profession. It competed with Denver-based schools, including University of Denver's Denver Medical College and Gross Medical College. In 1911, those institutions, which had combined in 1902, were struggling, unable to meet American Medical Association standards, and merged

Colorado General Hospital, circa 1930. *Denver Public Library, Western History Collection, X-28544; photograph by Glenn Mills.*

with CU's School of Medicine and Surgery. The following year, the school left Boulder, headquartering in downtown Denver at the former James B. Archer Mansion at 1307 Welton Street. These changes gave the school not only a faculty of respected physicians but also proximity to Denver's large City and County Hospital (today's Denver Health Medical Center), where students learned by practice.

The school grew rapidly, soon requiring a larger campus, and in 1920, university president George Norlin won a $750,000 grant from the Rockefeller Foundation to help build one. The bonanza was conditioned on CU finding matching funds and opening a hospital for patients who could not afford to pay. Money was found: the legislature passed a tax, the Denver Chamber of Commerce raised funds and individual and corporate philanthropists donated, including the Carnegie Foundation, Lawrence Phipps, the Berger-Kountze families, Charles Boettcher, Mary Reed, Daniels and Fisher Stores Company, The Denver Dry Goods Company, Gano-Downs Company, Fontius Shoe Company and others. Regents considered several sites; Frederick Bonfils's donation of seventeen acres between 8th and 9th Avenues, from Colorado Boulevard to Clermont Street, made the decision easier.

In 1924, the four-building campus opened to faculty, students and patients. Maurice B. Biscoe with William and Arthur Fisher designed the red brick buildings along Georgian Revival lines. The largest, facing 9th Avenue, was Colorado General Hospital, a four-story, multi-winged facility topped with a domed tower, with 150 inpatient beds, classrooms and laboratories. Its director, Dr. James J. Waring, had come to Colorado to cure his own tuberculosis, and under his leadership, the school gained a national reputation for the study and treatment of pulmonary ailments. Southeast of the medical hospital, the three-story Psychopathic Hospital had 80 beds; headed by Dr. Franklin G. Ebaugh, it treated Coloradans' mental health and became known for expertise in child psychiatry. (This was renamed the Psychiatric Hospital in 1952.) A three-story, 80-bed Nurses' Residence, northeast of Colorado General, faced 9th Avenue just west of Birch Street, with balconies on both ends along with first-floor classrooms and a lecture hall. The fourth building was a powerhouse and laundry. Underground tunnels connected all buildings. In 1935, the campus gained a fifth building, the Corinthian-columned Denison Memorial Medical Library, also designed by Biscoe, located near Colorado General's main entrance.

Despite chronic financial issues stemming from free healthcare and the legislature's chronic parsimony, the hospital and medical school grew, attracting patients from all over Colorado and students eager to learn from esteemed physicians. In 1967, one of them, Dr. Thomas E. Starzl, performed the world's first successful liver transplant. The buildings, particularly Colorado General, received numerous additions until it was clear that the original seventeen acres could not serve the hospital and medical school's needs much longer. Fortunately, CU obtained a golf driving range north of 9th Avenue in the 1930s and, by the early 1960s, was ready to build on it. James Quigg Newton Jr., Denver's mayor from 1947 to 1955, headed CU from 1956 through 1963, and he, with Governor Stephen L.R. McNichols, spearheaded the campus's transformation. In 1965, after nearly four years of construction, a massive new building opened. Designed by Robert G. Haselhuhn of Chicago's Schmidt, Garden and Erickson, the $22 million, eight-story facility housed 437 hospital beds in a large building north of 9th Avenue. Spanning that street, a five-story bridge connected with the 1925 building, which was converted to offices and laboratories. The structure's Modernist architecture was striking: the hospital and bridge were clad in vertical aluminum panels that pivoted through the day to mitigate Colorado's intense sunshine.

Aerial view of Colorado General Hospital and the University of Colorado Medical School campus, 1950; note the newly completed General Rose Memorial Hospital, *top*, and the under-construction Veterans Administration Hospital near it. *Denver Public Library, Western History Collection, X-23271; photograph by Dean Conger.*

Growth continued, with new buildings and wings filling in parking lots and lawns. Among these were the Belle Bonfils Memorial Blood Center (1953, Fisher and Fisher); the Webb-Waring Lung Institute (1955, designed by Denver's Robert Irwin); the School of Nursing (1966, Robert Irwin); the John F. Kennedy Child Development Center (1968, Denver's Victor Hornbein and Edward D. White Jr.); the School of Dentistry (1976, Robert Irwin); the Barbara Davis Center for Childhood Diabetes (1980, Denver's Davis Partnership); the eight-story Basic Research/Bioscience Building (1991, Davis Partnership); the Skaggs School of Pharmacy (1992, Denver's JH/P Partnership); and the eight-story Critical Care Tower (San Francisco's Stone, Marraccini & Patterson, 1996). Deserving special mention was the Colorado Children's Psychiatric Day Care Center (1962), designed in Frank Lloyd Wright–inspired Usonian style by Hornbein and White. Adjacent to the Psychiatric Hospital, this low-slung red brick structure with overhanging

University of Colorado Health Sciences Center bridge building across 9th Avenue, 2007. *Thomas J. Noel collection; photograph by K.C. Keefer.*

eaves and whimsical geometric design elements was meant to put children at ease. Preservationists strove to have it landmarked as an outstanding example of the architects' work but failed in their efforts.

By the 1990s, the campus was full. It needed to expand but ran into stiff opposition from nearby neighborhood associations and Denver mayor

Wellington E. Webb. The school and hospital (renamed in 1979 University of Colorado Health Sciences Center and University Hospital) therefore needed an entirely new site. It considered buying land at the recently closed Lowry Air Force Base and Stapleton International Airport, but entities controlling these sites would only sell land at full market value, which CU could not afford. In 1995, the Department of Defense announced the closure of Fitzsimons Army Medical Center, located on an expansive campus in Aurora. UCH president Dennis Brimhall and UCHSC chancellor Vincent Fulginiti were happy to listen to Fitzsimons's commander, Brigadier General John S. Parker's suggestion that they move there, and when the 227-acre site became available for the price of one dollar, the old campus's fate was sealed. CU acquired the Fitzsimons property in 1998 and opened its first buildings there in 2001. With large donations from Philip Anschutz, further construction at what was now called the Anschutz Medical Campus progressed rapidly. The hospital moved in 2007, and the pharmacy school, the last to relocate, left in 2011.

Denver, which could have kept the medical school's and hospital's thousands of jobs and associated economic activity had it matched the army's price for former airport land, was left with an empty campus. Frederick Bonfils's original land gift had stipulated medical and educational uses only, but the university eventually came to an agreement with the Bonfils Foundation. It also worked with the city to redevelop the campus in ways that would not conflict with Denver's goals and nearby residents' desires. Multiple developers presented plans. Preservationists and environmental sustainability advocates wondered why anything needed to be demolished, but every new developer insisted that purpose-built medical structures, even those constructed as recently as 1996, could not be economically converted to new use. Perhaps that is so, but much has been lost. In 2015, Continuum Partners bought the site, erecting a mixed-use project with high-density residential towers, shops, restaurants and a cinema. It left standing the 1924 Nurses' Residence, promising to convert it to residences (not yet begun at this book's writing). Continuum initially retained the 1965 bridge building across 9th Avenue, suggesting it might become a hotel, but changed its mind in 2018, and down it came.[42]

NOTES

Preface

1. Tom Junod, "Everything Is Different Now," *The Atlantic*, January 11, 2021, theatlantic.com/culture/archive/2021/01/everything-different-now/617633.
2. History Colorado, Denver Klan Ledgers, historycolorado.org/kkkledgers, vol. II, 10 (Campbell); 76 (Dutton); 175 (Reynolds); 213 (Ammons).

Introduction

3. Zeckendorf, *Autobiography*, 107–8, 115–16.

Chapter 1

4. Hosokawa, *Thunder*, 97–107; Carlo Davis, "A Symbolic Fight: Jefferson Park Scrape-Off Emblematic of Denver's Growth Debate," *Colorado Independent*, October 8, 2015, coloradoindependent.com/2015/10/08/denver-developer-and-history-buffs-feud-over-jefferson-park-home; Preserve the Anderson House, "History of the Anderson House," saveandersonhouse.wordpress.com/about/history-of-the-anderson-house.

5. Wilcox, *Lakewood-Colorado*, 91–96; Noel, "May Bonfils and Her Lost Belmar Mansion," 8–17.
6. Bretz, *Mansions*, 21, 108; Carr, *Queen of Denver*, 39; 50; Kohl, *Denver's Historic Mansions*, 220–23; Zimmer, *Denver's Capitol Hill*, 92; *Ballenger & Richards' Annual Denver City Directory*, 1893, 1894, 1896, 1899, 1900, 1915; *Colorado Evening Sun*, September 8, 1893; *Post*, June 22, 1902; July 25, 1902; September 5, 1902; December 23, 1902; January 27, 1903; January 29, 1903; June 5, 1904; June 6, 1904; June 10, 1904; June 14, 1904; June 18, 1904; June 20, 1904; June 22, 1904; July 2, 1904; July 7, 1904; July 10, 1904; July 11, 1904; July 13, 1904; August 16, 1904; August 20, 1904; August 22, 1904; August 24, 1904; August 25, 1904; August 26, 1904; August 27, 1904; September 14, 1904; September 15, 1904; October 4, 1904; October 5, 1904; October 10, 1904; December 18, 1904; January 12, 1905; January 13, 1905; November 19, 1905; December 27, 1908; *Times*, August 10, 1901; *Los Angeles Herald*, June 8, 1901; *New York Times*, January 12, 1905; March 3, 1958; *Pueblo Chieftan*, August 20, 1906; *News*, August 12, 1901; January 29, 1905; Find a Grave, "CPT William Decatur Bethell Sr.," findagrave.com/memorial/13461474/william-decatur-bethell#view-photo=161790920; Geni, "Capt. William Decator Bethell," geni.com/people/Capt-William-Bethell/6000000018952651049; Historic Maury County, "Hometown History," historicmaurycounty.com/2019/01/10/a-look-at-lost-landmarks-part-one; Wikipedia, "List of Mayors of Memphis, Tennessee," en.wikipedia.org/wiki/List_of_mayors_of_Memphis,_Tennessee. Note that Bethell spelled his name with two Ls; some relatives, including Louise Bethel Sneed, spelled it with one.
7. Lindell, "'No Greater Menace,'" 38–52; *Cervi's Journal*, July 17, 1952; *Post*, June 10, 1926; June 14, 1927; February 13, 1933; February 14, 1933; February 15, 1933; February 17, 1933; March 2, 1933; March 16, 1933; February 1, 1934; February 4, 1934; February 9, 1934; December 17, 1944; February 23, 1958; March 13, 1958; May 9, 1958; April 15, 1963; June 20, 1963; *News*, September 18, 1949; August 20, 1956; August 4, 1962; April 13, 1963; June 22, 1973.
8. Goodstein, *Ghosts of Denver*, 31–32; Noel and Norgren, *Denver: The City Beautiful*, 218; McMechen, "Brinton Terrace," 97–114; *Republican*, September 12, 1883; *Post*, January 13, 1907; October 13, 1907; September 6, 1908; June 2, 1912; April 13, 1914; May 26, 1917; June 1, 1919; February 11, 1928; October 16, 1932; May 16, 1940; *News*, March 18, 1880; May 19, 1892; May 7, 1908; November 5, 1911; April 27, 1912; February 19, 1914; March 1, 1914; August 12, 1917; December

21, 1919; January 25, 1920; December 7, 1922; *Leadville Democrat*, January 1, 1884; Find a Grave, "William Shaw Ward," www.findagrave.com/memorial/33815205/william-shaw-ward; Modernist West, "John Edward Thompson," www.modernistwest.com/john-e-thompson-m.

9. Goodstein, *Ghosts of Denver*, 88–89; Kohl, *Denver's Historic Mansions*, 33–38; Stone, *History of Colorado*, Vol. 1, 671; *Denver Municipal Facts*, June 26, 1909; *Post*, September 10, 1898; January 5, 1899; January 6, 1899; August 16, 1899; October 3, 1899; October 6, 1899; December 19, 1906; February 26, 1907; September 13, 1908; October 16, 1918; August 10, 1919; September 17, 1919; November 11, 1919; April 4, 1943; May 23, 1963; *News*, April 10, 1881; January 20, 1882; January 29, 1888; March 12, 1889; January 1, 1891; February 14, 1892; July 11, 1893; February 24, 1894; December 17, 1894; May 8, 1898; August 12, 1899; November 26, 1909; April 27, 1961; August 17, 1961; Knights of Columbus, "Our History," kofc539denver.org/our-history; Wikipedia, "Elwell Stephen Otis," wikipedia.org/wiki/Elwell_Stephen_Otis; Denver building permit (1889) 12-24.00#1890.00; National Register of Historic Places Registration Form for Fuller Granville House, Aurora, CO.

10. Noel and Norgren, *Denver: The City Beautiful*, 203–5; *Historic Denver News* 45, no. 4 (Fall 2016): 3; Meeting Record, Landmark Preservation Commission, October 18, 2016, denvergov.org/content/dam/denvergov/Portals/646/documents/landmark/lpc/meeting_records/2016/101816_LPC_meeting_record.FINAL.pdf; Erica Meltzer, "An Effort to Preserve a Queen Anne in Denver's Jefferson Park Fails," Denverite, November 21, 2016, denverite.com/2016/11/21/denver-preserve-queen-anne-jefferson-park-fails; web.archive.org/web/20160721213715/; historycolorado.org/sites/default/files/files/OAHP/Guides/Architects_hoytb.pdf.

11. Noel and Hanson, *Park Hill Neighborhood*, 7–11, 70; Cherokee Ranch, "History," cherokeeranch.org/history.html; denvergov.org/content/dam/denvergov/Portals/646/documents/landmark/designations/Proposed_Designations/1980_Albion_St_Landmark_Designation_Application.pdf; Historic Denver, "1980 Albion—The Hut," historicdenver.org/1980-albion-the-hut.

12. Bakemeier, *Country Club Heritage*, 120–23; Kohl, *Denver's Historic Mansions*, 202–8; Kreck, *Murder at the Brown Palace*, 69, 78; Noel, *Richthofen's Montclair*, 53, 74–75; *Post*, December 12, 1895; May 7, 1905; December 22, 1906; December 24, 1906; December 10, 1907; January 28, 1908; April 20, 1908; August 26, 1909; December 17, 1909; January 23, 1910; October 3, 1912; June 20, 1918; July 30, 1918; October 24,

1927; December 20, 1935; *News*, February 8, 1891; May 12, 1893; August 27, 1909; June 21, 1918.

13. Corbett & Ballenger's annual *Denver City Directory*, 1896; *Denver Householder's Directory*, 1937; *Colorado Springs Gazette*, September 14, 1919; *Post*, September 14, 1895; October 20, 1905; August 24, 1906; April 12, 1908; December 1, 1909; October 7, 1910; November 12, 1910; August 31, 1911; September 4, 1915; January 12, 1916; January 13, 1916; April 11, 1916; June 16, 1916; March 26, 1917; May 11, 1917; *News*, September 23, 1889; November 10, 1889; March 6, 1892; May 13, 1893; November 10, 1893; April 29, 1894; August 7, 1898; November 8, 1905; December 3, 1905; December 10, 1905; April 4, 1906; August 25, 1906; January 30, 1907; April 16, 1907; April 23, 1907; February 2, 1908; September 12, 1909; April 5, 1911; October 4, 1911; December 23, 1913; January 8, 1914; April 5, 1916; *San Diego Union*, July 28, 1931; Denver Building Permits 1889–1906, p. 98, permit (1890)-19.00#1702.00; milb.com/milb/history.top100.jsp; Wikipedia, "George E. Smith (gambler)," wikipedia.org/wiki/George_E_Smith_(gambler); Wikipedia, "Western League (1900–1958)," wikipedia.org/wiki/Western_League_(1900-1958); Colorado Architects Biographical Sketch, "Balcomb, Robert G.," historycolorado.org/sites/default/files/media/documents/2018/architects_balcomb.pdf.

14. Wiberg, *Rediscovering Northwest Denver*, 118; Mattes, "Informal History of the Denver Westerners," 3; *Post*, September 11, 1911; June 16, 1914; April 30, 1916; September 30, 1932; *News*, April 13, 1910; May 7, 1910; June 26, 1910; March 30, 1922; December 12, 1922; *Denver Householders' Directory and Street and Avenue Guide*, vol. 3, 1927, and vol. 4, 1928; Denver Building Permit (1905) 3-27.00#512.00; Denver Landmarks Preservation Commission, Application for Certificate of Non-Historic Status, #30-08 2008Q00015; decennial U.S. censuses, 1910 and 1920; Ray Defa, email to author, March 7, 2021.

Chapter 2

15. Brettell, *Historic Denver*, 40–42; Harry E. Kelsey Jr., "Finis P. Ernest," *Colorado Magazine* 31, no. 4 (October 1954): 290–99; *Post*, December 26, 1906; March 31, 1908; June 4, 1910; June 27, 1912; July 4, 1912; *News*, July 2, 1886; August 29, 1890; November 29, 1891; February 9, 1898; October 28, 1909; June 21, 1912; June 28, 1912; June 30, 1912; January 9, 1921; October 25, 1959; Find a Grave, "William Henry Harrison

'Bill' Cranmer," findagrave.com/memorial/67285081/william-henry_harrison-cranmer. Harry Kelsey's article is based on extensive interviews with George Ernest Cranmer.

16. Brettell, *Historic Denver*, 42; *Cervi's Rocky Mountain Journal*, May 20, 1970; *Post*, April 5, 1908; April 25, 1909; February 8, 1913; April 12, 1913; March 31, 1918; April 16, 1919; May 21, 1919; December 17, 1922; April 8, 1923; May 16, 1923; August 28, 1923; August 29, 1923; December 17, 1923; April 21, 1924; April 26, 1924; June 1, 1924; November 15, 1925; February 27, 1935; June 26, 1967; February 1, 1970; June 3, 1970; November 15, 1970; October 19, 1971; *News*, November 7, 1901; April 25, 1909; January 13, 1911; April 2, 1969; June 3, 1970; May 14, 1972; *Times*, July 2, 1902.

17. Brettell, *Historic Denver*, 53; Goodstein, *Robert Speer's Denver*, 381; Robinson and Cafky, *Denver's Street Railways*, vol. 2, 77; Smiley, *History of Denver*, 962–63; *News*, January 1, 1896; April 8, 1910; April 11, 1915; June 19, 1976; June 29, 1978; *Post*, July 3, 1910; February 18, 1977; June 25, 1978; *Republican*, April 21, 1900; *Times*, July 23, 1898; March 10, 1901; December 2, 1901.

18. Smiley, *History of Denver*, 576, 842; Copeland, "Mining Stock Exchanges," 68–74, 78–82; Mumey, "Prospector's Statue Atop Mining Exchange Building," 117–24; *Cervi's Rocky Mountain Journal*, June 19, 1963; *Post*, September 14, 1949; March 15, 1953; November 24, 1958; November 11, 1962; September 3, 1968; *News*, August 17, 1963.

19. Noel and Norgren, *Denver: The City Beautiful*, 123, 136; *Denver Municipal Facts*, January–February 1928, 17; *Cervi's Journal*, March 12, 1958; *Post*, August 4, 1912; August 24, 1934; May 24, 1964; February 17, 1983; *News*, September 24, 1925; January 1, 1981; February 3, 1981; February 17, 1983; *Westword*, May 14, 1981.

20. Hopkins misquoted Kingsley slightly, substituting "the" for "their" in front of "earth." After the Tabor's demolition, Central City Opera received the curtain. Too large for their stage, they stored it in a building with a leaking roof. In 1982, finding it ruined, they sent it to the Central City dump, where it was burned (*News*, January 29, 1984).

21. Barrett and Barrett, *High Drama*, 14–18, 51–63; Johnson, *Denver's Old Theater Row*, 42–47; Moynihan, *Augusta Tabor*, 76–77; Noel, *City and the Saloon*, 92; Noel and Zimmer, *Showtime*, 25–28; Smith, *Horace Tabor*, 260–62; *Post*, September 4, 1957; January 9, 1964; *Times*, June 7, 1899; *News*, January 1, 1881; September 2, 1881; September 4, 1881; September 6, 1881; June 18, 1933; January 24, 1963.

Chapter 3

22. Smiley, *History*, 844; *Colorado Sun*, July 3, 1892; July 7, 1892; *Times*, January 6, 1899; September 3, 1900; January 26, 1902; April 2, 1902; *News*, May 3, 1874; February 2, 1876; August 30, 1885.
23. *Post*, November 4, 1911; November 5, 1911; November 6, 1911; November 7, 1911; *Republican*, January 1, 1907; *Times*, December 1, 1901; August 13, 1903, January 1, 1911; *News*, January 17, 1912; August 1, 1912.
24. *Colorado Labor Advocate*, June 4, 1946; *Post*, July 9, 1948; November 17, 1949; August 6, 1950; September 27, 1950; November 8, 1986; October 27, 1995; *News*, June 21, 1931; October 17, 1938; *Mines Magazine* 85, no. 5 (September/October 1998).
25. *Post*, October 15, 1901; December 31, 1911; January 29, 1914; September 22, 1922; July 18, 1924; May 31, 1925; May 18, 1926; November 25, 1926; January 7, 1927; April 10, 1927; April 9, 1928; July 17, 1928; December 4, 1928; June 12, 1930; September 9, 1933; September 25, 1935; October 13, 1937; June 2, 1960; October 16, 1960; *News*, July 15, 1906; January 29, 1911; December 17, 1911; January 30, 1912; Denver Public Library, "Davis & Shaw Furniture Company," history.denverlibrary.org/news/davis-shaw-furniture-company-denver's-20th-century-furniture-store-0; *Furniture World*, "106-Year-Old Denver Store Davis & Shaw Conducts Successful GOB Sale," August 4, 2005, furninfo.com/furniture-industry-news-archive/5327.
26. Corbett & Ballenger's annual *Denver City Directory* (1900, 1905, 1907, 1911, 1923); *Post*, February 28, 1896; June 4, 1940; August 21, 1962; December 12, 1965; September 4, 1966; May 29, 1986; *News*, June 2, 1923.
27. *Post*, January 10, 1922; December 12, 1924; *News*, December 19, 1924; April 1, 1933.
28. Vickers, *History of Denver*, 368–71, 487–88; *Post*, February 19, 1903; March 29, 1903; May 16, 1903; August 21, 1909; February 5, 1917; October 29, 1925; January 19, 1930; September 18, 1931; January 17, 1933; February 4, 1933; January 10, 1934; May 24, 1934; September 9, 1934; October 8, 1934; May 12, 1935; May 19, 1937; March 10, 1938; June 26, 1970; *Times*, March 4, 1903; *News*, July 12, 1885; January 23, 1887; July 12, 1891; September 13, 1908; August 21, 1909; February 5, 1917; May 18, 1919; January 10, 1963; August 29, 1965; Jonathan Ambrosino, "English Influence and How It Reached Denver Organs, 1925–1940," jambrosino.neocities.org/lecture-ohs1998.html; Denver

building permit 1891-14-27.00#522.00; Denver building permit 1903-4-16.00#554.00.

29. The Hughes Block came down at this time for the five-story Neusteter Company store, which remains standing.

30. *News*, December 12, 1960; Kress Foundation, "Our Story," kressfoundation.org/about/kress_legacy; National Building Museum, "S.H. Kress & Company Collection," nbm.org/collections/s-h-kress-company; nbm.org/exhibits/past/2000_1996/Kress/Traveling.

31. *Columbus [OH] Dispatch*, June 4, 1980; December 5, 1982; *Greensboro [NC] Record*, February 22, 1984; February 23, 1995; May 19, 1995; *Post*, August 14, 1938; August 21, 1938; *News*, February 13, 1943; April 7, 1983; June 14, 1990; April 28, 1992; December 28, 1994; Four and Twenty, "The Skinny—Montaldo's," blackbirdantiques.blogspot.com/2013/11/the-skinny-montaldos.html.

Chapter 4

32. Smiley, *History*, 458–59, 782, 954; Marguerite Riordan, Papers, Denver Public Library Western History Collection, WH1094, Box 6, FF19, "Daniels and Fishers" [*sic*], unpublished manuscript, 23.

33. Dallas, *Cherry Creek Gothic*, 85; *Post*, December 21, 1902; December 24, 1902; December 31, 1903; *News*, April 25, 1865; August 28, 1865; September 21, 1865; May 5, 1869; January 15, 1870; November 30, 1870; May 5, 1871; August 20, 1872; October 2, 1873; October 19, 1875; December 17, 1902; April 23, 1909; Amazing Black History, "Ford, Barney L.—Pioneer of Colorado," amazingblackhistory.com/2019/02/13/ford-barney-l-pioneer-of-colorado; Colorado Encyclopedia, "Barney Ford," coloradoencyclopedia.org/article/barney-ford; History Colorado, "Barney Ford: African American Pioneer," historycolorado.org/story/collections-library/2017/02/08/barney-ford-african-american-pioneer; United States decennial censuses for 1860, 1870 and 1900.

34. Smiley, *History of Denver*, 616; *Post*, September 9, 1903; May 9, 1904; September 29, 1904; January 22, 1905; March 26, 1905; April 11, 1905; January 5, 1907; May 31, 1907; May 7, 1914; May 9, 1914; July 27, 1914; July 29, 1914; July 31, 1914; August 6, 1914; July 12, 1915; November 13, 1916; June 23, 1921; September 12, 1924; December 12, 1924; September 27, 1925; November 29, 1925; November 28, 1926; September 30, 1937; March 7, 1954; April 20, 1957; January 8, 1970;

October 31, 1977; February 10, 1991; June 12, 2000; *News*, April 4, 1897; October 1, 1897; April 1, 1902; October 5, 1902; April 17, 1904; April 6, 1906; May 26, 1914; January 6, 1916; May 26, 1916; July 20, 1918; March 9, 1958; April 26, 1963; October 20, 1968; May 24, 1998; Denver Building Permits 1888–1905, 282, 284, 316; Wikipedia, "Carl Lotave," wikipedia.org/wiki/Carl_Lotave.

35. Arps, *Denver in Slices*, 142–54; Dallas, *No More Than Five*, 98–105; Fowler, *Timberline*, 45; Hosokawa, *Thunder in the Rockies*, 33; Kerouac, *On the Road*, 264; Noel, *Denver's Larimer Street*, 142–47; Smith, *Horace Tabor*, 151, 212.

Chapter 5

36. Ballard, Bond and Paxton, *Lowry Air Force Base*, 9, 104; Carroll E. Edson and W.H. Bergtold, "The Agnes Memorial Sanitarium," *Transactions of the American Clinical and Climatological Association* 20 (1904): 164–78; *Post*, April 26, 1903; May 10, 1903; May 25, 1903; April 24, 1904; June 5, 1904; July 3, 1904; October 26, 1904; Lowry Foundation, "Building 256," lowryfoundation.org/lowry-legacy/buildings/buildings-index/building-256.

37. Goodstein, *Robert Speer's Denver*, 33–39; Lindsey and O'Higgins, *The Beast*, xi–xxxv, 75, 149; Smiley, *History of Denver*, 541, 543–44; *News*, January 14, 1880; January 31, 1880; February 1, 1880; February 3, 1880; May 19, 1880; June 25, 1881; January 20, 1933; *Post*, June 9, 1918; October 12, 1919; January 1, 1928; January 31, 1932; December 30, 1932; January 1, 1933; December 3, 1933; December 6, 1933; December 26, 1933; November 24, 1974; *Republican*, April 18, 1883; November 24, 1912.

38. Leonard and Noel, *Denver: Mining Camp to Metropolis*, 105–6, 128; Perkin, *First Hundred Years*, 387–88; Smiley, *History of Denver*, 647, 920–27; *Frank Leslie's Illustrated Newspaper*, May 19, 1883; *Denver Tribune*, January 1, 1880; *News*, April 21, 1882; May 24, 1884; July 13, 1946; *Rocky Mountain Herald*, February 3, 1973.

39. Goodstein, *Haunts of Washington Park*, 233–37; McGinn, *A Wide-Awake Woman*, 19; Van Wyke, *Town of South Denver*, 124.

40. Goodstein, *North Side Story*, 60–61, 238–41; Smiley, *History of Denver*, 775–76; *Post*, December 10, 1933; May 27, 1943; April 18, 1951; *Republican*, September 15, 1896; October 27, 1903; *Times*, January 5, 1902; September 3, 1902; November 19, 1902; October 26, 1903; *News*, February 7, 1896; February 19, 1934; March 27, 1934; July 22, 1934; June 15, 1941; August

19, 1942; February 4, 1943; May 28, 1943; September 15, 1978; April 3, 1983; FamilySearch.org/tree/pedigree/fanchart/L79N-YLH.

41. Goodstein, *North Side Story*, 12–831; Zahller, *Italy in Colorado*, 220–23; *Post*, April 4, 1967; May 27, 1969; August 3, 1973; Mother Cabrini Shrine, mothercabrinishrine.org.

42. Noel, *University of Colorado Hospital*, 8, 22, 32, 34–36, 38–39, 43–44, 47–48, 51, 56–58, 67–68, 70–71, 86–99; Thomas Gounley, "Bridge over 9th Avenue, Remnant of Former CU Hospital Campus, to Be Demolished," BusinessDen, December 11, 2018, businessden.com/2018/12/11/bridge-over-9th-avenue-remnant-of-former-cu-hospital-campus-to-be-demolished; University of Colorado Anschutz Medical Campus, "The History of CU School of Medicine," medschool.cuanschutz.edu/deans-office/about-us/our-history; University of Colorado–Denver, "Institutional Planning," ucdenver.edu/about/departments/InstitutionalPlanning/CampusPlanning/Documents/Former%209th%20Avenue%20and%20Colorado%20Boulevard%20Campus.pdf.

BIBLIOGRAPHY

Books

Bakemeier, Alice Millett. *Country Club Heritage: A History and Guide to a Denver Neighborhood.* Denver, CO: Country Club Historic Neighborhood, Inc., 2000.

Ballard, Jack Stokes, John Bond and George Paxton. *Lowry Air Force Base.* Charleston, SC: Arcadia Publishing, 2013.

Barrett, Daniel, and Beth R. Barrett. *High Drama: Colorado's Historic Theatres.* Montrose, CO: Western Reflections Publishing Company, 2005.

Brettell, Richard R. *Historic Denver: The Architects and the Architecture.* Denver, CO: Historic Denver, Inc., 1973.

Bretz, James. *Mansions of Denver: The Vintage Years 1870–1938.* Boulder, CO: Pruett Publishing Company, 2005.

Carr, Shelby. *The Queen of Denver: Louise Sneed Hill and the Emergence of Modern High Society.* Charleston, SC: The History Press, 2020.

Cuba, Stan. *The Denver Artists Guild: Its Founding Members, an Illustrated History.* Denver: History Colorado, 2015.

Dallas, Sandra. *Cherry Creek Gothic: Victorian Architecture in Denver.* Norman: University of Oklahoma Press, 1971.

———. *No More Than Five in a Bed: Colorado Hotels in the Old Days.* Norman: University of Oklahoma Press, 1967.

Finch, F. ("Doc Bird"). *Members of the Denver Traffic Club in Caricature.* Denver, CO: Finch & Sowers Publishers, 1909.

Fowler, Gene. *Timberline: A Story of Bonfils and Tammen*. Repr., Garden City, NY: Garden City Books, 1951.

Goodstein, Phil. *The Ghosts of Denver: Capitol Hill*. Denver, CO: New Social Publications, 1996.

———. *The Haunts of Washington Park*. Denver, CO: New Social Publications, 2009.

———. *North Side Story*. Denver, CO: New Social Publications, 2011.

———. *Robert Speer's Denver, 1904–1920: The Mile High City in the Progressive Era*. Denver, CO: New Social Publications, 2004.

Hosokawa, Bill. *Thunder in the Rockies: The Incredible Denver Post*. New York: William Morrow, 1976.

Johnson, Forrest H. *Denver's Old Theater Row: The Story of Curtis Street and Its Glamorous Show Business.* Denver, CO: Gem Publications, 1970.

Kerouac, Jack. *On the Road*. New York: Penguin Books, 1976 reprint.

Kohl, Edith Eudora. *Denver's Historic Mansions*. Denver, CO: Sage Books, 1957.

Kreck, Dick. *Murder at the Brown Palace*. Golden, CO: Fulcrum Publishing, 2003.

Leonard, Stephen J., and Thomas J. Noel. *Denver: Mining Camp to Metropolis*. Niwot: University Press of Colorado, 1990.

Lindsey, Benjamin Barr, and Harvey J. O'Higgins. *The Beast*. New York: Doubleday, Page & Company, 1910; reprinted 2009 by University Press of Colorado (Niwot, CO), with a foreword by Stephen J. Leonard.

McGinn, Elinor. *A Wide-Awake Woman: Josephine Roche in the Era of Reform*. Denver: Colorado Historical Society, 2002.

Noel, Thomas J. *The City and the Saloon: Denver 1858–1916*. Lincoln: University of Nebraska Press, 1982.

———. *Denver's Larimer Street: Main Street, Skid Row and Urban Renaissance*. Denver, CO: Historic Denver, Inc., 1981.

———. *Richthofen's Montclair: A Pioneer Denver Suburb*. Boulder, CO: Pruett Publishing Company, 1978.

———. *University of Colorado Hospital: A History*. Aurora: University of Colorado Hospital Foundation, 2012.

Noel, Thomas J., and Amy B. Zimmer. *Showtime: Denver's Performing Arts, Convention Centers & Theatre District.* Denver, CO: Division of Theatres & Arenas, 2008.

Noel, Thomas J., and Barbara S. Norgren. *Denver: The City Beautiful.* Denver, CO: Historic Denver, Inc., 1987.

Noel, Thomas J., and William J. Hansen. *The Park Hill Neighborhood*. Denver, CO: Historic Denver, Inc., 2002.

Perkin, Robert L. *The First Hundred Years: An Informal History of Denver and the* Rocky Mountain News. Garden City, NY: Doubleday & Company, Inc., 1959.

Robertson, Don, and Reverend W. Morris Cafky. *Denver's Street Railways*. Vol. 2, *1901–1950*. Denver, CO: Sundance Publications, Ltd., 2004.

Smiley, Jerome C. *History of Denver*. Denver, CO: Sun-Times Publishing Company, 1901.

Smith, Duane. *Horace Tabor: His Life and the Legend*. Boulder, CO: Pruett Publishing Company, 1981.

Stone, Wilbur Fisk, ed. *History of Colorado*. Vol. 1. Chicago: S.J. Clarke Publishing Company, 1918.

Van Wyke, Millie. *The Town of South Denver: Its People, Neighborhoods and Events Since 1858*. Boulder, CO: Pruett Publishing Co., 1991.

Vickers, W.B. *History of the City of Denver, Arapahoe County and Colorado*. Chicago: O.L. Baskin & Company, 1880.

Wilcox, Patricia K., ed. *Lakewood-Colorado: An Illustrated Biography*. Lakewood, CO: Lakewood 25th Birthday Commission, 1994.

Zahller, Alisa. *Italy in Colorado: Family Histories from Denver and Beyond.* Virginia Beach, VA: Donning Company, Publishers, 2008.

Zeckendorf, William, with Edward McCreary. *The Autobiography of William Zeckendorf*. New York: Holt, Rinehart and Winston, 1970.

Zimmer, Amy B. *Denver's Capitol Hill*. Charleston, SC: Arcadia Publishing, 2009.

Articles

Copeland, James B. "Mining Stock Exchanges and Financing the Colorado Mining Industry: 1864–1900." *The Mining History Journal* (2013): 68–93.

Lindell, Lisa. "'No Greater Menace': Verne Sankey and the Kidnapping of Charles Boettcher II." Hilton M. Briggs Library Faculty Publications, Paper 30, 2004. openprairie.sdstate.edu/library_pubs/30.

McMechen, Edgar C. "Brinton Terrace." *The Colorado Magazine* 14, no. 3 (May 1947): 97–114.

Mumey, Noley. "Prospector's Statue Atop Mining Exchange Building." *The Colorado Magazine* 39 no. 2 (April 1962): 117–24.

Noel, Thomas J. "May Bonfils and Her Lost Belmar Mansion." *Colorado Heritage* (Fall 2018): 8–17.

Online Sources

Brantigan, Charles O., ed. "The Denver Building Permits File, Volume IV: The Denver Building Permits File, 1889–1905." digital.denverlibrary.org/digital/collection/p16079coll8/id/1708/rec/1.

———. "The Denver Building Permits File, Volume VII: The Denver Building Permits File, 1906–1914." digital.denverlibrary.org/digital/collection/p16079coll8/id/85/rec/5.

Websites as noted in endnotes.

INDEX

E

F

G

H

I

J

K

L

M

R

S

Z

ABOUT THE AUTHOR

Denver native Mark A. Barnhouse, currently residing in northwest Denver, has been fascinated by his city's history from an early age. A graduate of the University of Colorado–Denver, he has researched and written about Denver's history for twenty-five years. His most recent books include *Tattered Cover Book Store: A Storied History*, *A History Lover's Guide to Denver* and *Lost Department Stores of Denver*; see ArcadiaPublishing.com for a full listing. He is available for talks and is a member of one of Denver's oldest history groups, the Denver Posse of Westerners. You'll find him on Facebook at "Denver History Books by Mark A. Barnhouse."